Guide to the Federal Taxation of California Registered Domestic Partners and Same-Sex Married Couples

For Use in Preparation of 2010 Tax Returns

Marci A. Flanery, CPA, PhD

Marci Flanery

Table of Contents

Acknowledgements

My heartfelt thanks go to the many people who helped me with this project. First of all, my thanks go to Rob Thesman who not only encouraged me to write this Guide but also served as a patient advisor and sounding board on the technical aspects of RDP taxation. Second, thanks go to Patty Roberts for editing the original draft of the Guide for spelling and grammatical errors. Any remaining errors are mine, not hers. Finally, I thank Bob Lane for introducing me to RDP taxation and Karen Stogdill for the opportunity to learn from and work with her RDP and same-sex married clients during the busy season of 2011.

Disclaimer

Statement required by the U.S. Internal Revenue Service and Circular 230

This book has not been written with the intention of providing tax advice. It was written to provide a guide to many of the U.S. and California income tax issues that confront California State Registered Domestic Partners and Same-Sex Married Couples. Tax advice can only occur in a professional relationship where your professional advisor has all of the facts necessary to arrive at a proper conclusion. Accordingly, this book cannot be relied upon to avoid penalties or to be used to promote ideas to another taxpayer.

The ideas and information in this book are very general. The U.S. tax laws change every day with new pronouncements by the Internal Revenue Service, the U.S. court system and the lawmakers. The primary objective of this book is to help you understand and comply with the U.S. tax rules without overpaying or underpaying the taxes that would be due.

Foreword

DON'T PANIC[1]

This excellent advice applies wherever you are in the galaxy and in particular if you are registered domestic partners about to prepare your US and California Income Tax returns. Because the Guide is meant to be comprehensive, it includes topics that will not apply to the average California registered domestic partner/same-sex married couple, so don't be intimidated by the length. In fact, if your returns consist only of wages, a little bit of interest or dividend income and a mortgage interest deduction, they will be pretty easy, and this Guide should be all you need to help you properly prepare your return for filing with the IRS.

The best additional advice I can give you is to simply take preparation of your tax return one step at a time. For instance, gather your W-2's and then, as you read the section on reporting wages, substitute your actual numbers into the examples. Once you've done that, tackle the next item on your list - maybe dividends and interest - on the next day using the same technique. Don't enter anything into your tax preparation program until you've completed this same step for all of your income and deduction items. Breaking your return into pieces and knowing in advance what the numbers should end up being before you enter them on your real tax return will make it a lot easier and less confusing for you.

Finally, if in the end you find completing your tax returns too confusing, too stressful, or too time consuming, hire a professional who has experience preparing these kinds of returns. I have a friend who refers to hiring a CPA to prepare his return as "an affordable luxury." If you've read through the Guide, you will have a good general understanding of what should be reported on you and your partner's tax return, and you can leave the details to the professional while you get to enjoy your weekends.

Whatever you decide to do with regard to your tax return preparation, I hope this Guide helps you to gain a better understanding of the new reporting requirements.

Best Regards,

Marci Flanery, CPA

---

[1] Douglas Adams, The Hitchhiker's Guide to the Galaxy

Introduction & Background

Changes in Tax Reporting for 2010

2010 was an important year for registered domestic partners living in the community property states of California, Washington, and Nevada. In May of 2010, the Chief Counsel to the Internal Revenue Service published a memorandum, referred to as CCA 201021050 throughout this Guide and reproduced in Appendix A, making it clear that California registered domestic partners must split community income in preparing their 2010 tax returns. In addition, since the change in California community property law that resulted in splitting community income took effect January 1, 2007, the memorandum also stated that California registered domestic partners and same-sex married couples have the option of amending their 2007, 2008 and 2009 tax returns to properly reflect community income in accordance with CCA 201021050.

Although the IRS memorandum specifically refers to California registered domestic partners, the information it contains holds for couples in any state that recognizes registered domestic partnerships and/or same-sex marriages; is a community property law state; and extends the state community property laws to the earned income (not just property) of the couple.

At this time, the only states other than California whose residents currently meet these requirements are Washington and Nevada. Community property rights were extended to the income of Washington State Registered Domestic Partners as of June 12, 2008, and Nevada is the latest state to extend community property rights to its registered domestic partners with an effective date of October 1, 2009. Unlike those of California, however, state laws in Washington and Nevada, do not extend to same-sex married couples the same recognition as that granted to registered domestic partners, and so the new filing requirements only apply to registered domestic partners in those states.

The application of community property law to RDPs is actually based on an 80-year-old court case, Poe v. Seaborn (1930), in which a married couple domiciled in Washington State split the husband's income, reporting one-half on the husband's tax return and one-half on the wife's tax return (the tax law allowing married taxpayers to file joint tax returns did not exist until after Poe v. Seaborn was litigated). Because the couple lived in a community property state and the wife had a right to one-half of the husband's community income, the courts found that the income was properly reported one-half by each spouse. Reporting in this way resulted in a lower combined tax for the couple. The situation in the Poe v. Seaborn case, two individuals covered by community property rules and not able to file a joint tax return, is similar to that of RDPs/SSMCs living in states that extend community property rights to them while they are still required to file separate federal tax returns.

Splitting Community Income May Result in Lower Taxes

Most RDP couples I've talked to lament the fact that they are now required to file tax returns based on their community property rights. However, although RDPs may be correct in stating that their returns are more complicated to prepare than under the Pre-CCA 201021050 rules, there can be a significant tax advantage to this filing method when there is an income disparity between the two partners.

Furthermore, this tax advantage *is not* available to opposite-sex married couples so, at least in this instance, the conjunction of California community property law with US tax law may actually lead to a more favorable tax result for many RDPs.

Is it worth a few extra hours of your time each year or the cost of hiring a CPA to reduce your combined taxes by $2,000, $8,000, or even as much as $25,000? Although some RDPs will not benefit from the new rules, many will. For instance, the chart below illustrates the combined tax savings for RDPs Bartok and Hobart when they split their community property income. In the example, Bartok is assumed to have wages of $250,000. The tax savings to the couple will depend on Hobart's earnings, which we have varied in this example from a low of $0 to a high of $200,000.

Combined Tax Savings
Bartok Earns $250,000

	Hobart Earns $0	Hobart Earns $50,000	Hobart Earns $100,000	Hobart Earns $150,000	Hobart Earns $200,000
■ Tax Savings	$12,349	$4,239	$3,440	$1,560	$0

When Hobart has net income of zero and Bartok has net income of $250,000 (left column in chart), the combined tax savings to the couple are $12,349. By contrast, when Hobart has income of $200,000 and Bartok has net income of $250,000 (right column in chart) the combined tax savings to the couple are zero.

Tax savings from splitting community property income are due to the progressive nature of the US tax rates. In 2010, taxpayers filing under the Single status paid a lower rate of tax on the first $373,650 of taxable income. When RDPs have disparate incomes - as in the first scenario in which Hobart has income of zero and Bartok has income of $250,000, the new income-splitting rule allows both taxpayers to benefit from the low marginal rates. Without income splitting, Hobart is taxed on zero income at the lowest rates and Bartok's US tax is $64,531, an average rate of almost 26%. With income splitting, Hobart and Bartok will each pay tax of $26,091 on their share of the reported income for a total combined tax of $52,182 saving them $12,349 (combined tax liability without income splitting of $64,531 versus combined tax liability with income splitting of $52,182). In a more extreme example (not illustrated above), when one partner earns $1,000,000 and the other earns $0, the tax savings can be as much as $25,834. Moreover, this is not a one-time tax savings. RDPs can benefit from income splitting every year.

Planning Point

Amending Your Prior Year Returns and the Statute of Limitations

CCA 201021050 requires California RDPs/SSMCs to file their 2010 tax returns reporting each partner's share of community property income. CCA 201021050 also allows - but does not require - taxpayers to amend prior years' tax returns. Since California changed its community property rules to apply to RDPs/SSMCs effective January 1, 2007 taxpayers may amend their 2007, 2008 and 2009 tax returns. Due to the 3-year statute of limitations, if you filed your 2008 tax return on or before April 15, 2009 (the original due date) you must make the decision to amend and file the amended 2008 tax return prior to April 15, 2012. Amended returns for 2009 will be due April 15, 2013. If your 2007 tax return was filed by April 15, 2008, the statute has already expired for 2007 tax returns. If you extended your 2007 tax return, the latest possible date to amend the tax return would be October 15, 2010.

Qualifying as a California RDP

To qualify as an RDP, you must meet certain requirements. FTB Publication 737 defines a domestic partnership as a civil contract between two adults who meet these additional statutory requirements:

1. either both persons are members of the same sex or at least one person is sixty-two years of age or older and meets requirements for Social Security old age insurance benefits;
2. both persons share a common residence;
3. neither person is married to someone other than the party to the domestic partnership, and neither person is in a domestic partnership with another person;
4. the two persons are not related by blood in a way that would prevent them from being married to each other in California;
5. both persons are at least eighteen years old;
6. both persons are capable of consenting to the domestic partnership; and
7. the individuals must file a Declaration of Domestic Partnership with the California Secretary of State.

In addition, the FTB instructions state that if you have entered into a same-sex legal union (other than marriage) in another state and that union is substantially equivalent to a California registered domestic partnership you are required to file a California income tax return using either the Married/RDP filing joint or Married/RDP filing separate status.

As discussed in the next section, registering as an RDP can have a profound impact on the legal rights that each partner has with respect to earnings and property acquired after registration. This Guide is not legal advice and should not be used as a substitute for obtaining competent legal advice.

Community Property vs. Separate Property

The first step in preparing your tax return is to determine the character of all income earned and property owned by you and your partner. Every RDP/SSMC couple should complete a worksheet that they update at least annually to identify and track their community property (CP) and their separate property (SP). Appendix C includes an example of a CP/SP worksheet that you can use to document your personal assets. Couples should complete this worksheet together to assure that 1) all assets are listed and 2) that the partners agree on the characterization of the assets. The IRS publishes Publication 555 (Appendix B) to assist couples to understand how to make the CP/SP characterization. In addition, consultation with an attorney in the first year that RDP/SSMC couples complete this worksheet is advisable.

Community Property and Community Income - General Rules

California is a community property state. In general, this means that income earned and property acquired during your domestic partnership belongs to both of the partners. California RDPs and SSMC acquired community property rights as of January 1, 2007.

Community **property** will generally include

1. property acquired after you registered as RDPs while domiciled in a community property state;
2. property that you and your partner agree to convert from separate to community property (See following section on gift taxes); and
3. property that cannot be identified as separate property (See the Planning Point: Separate means Separate, below)

Community **income** will generally include

1. income from community property (see above);
2. wages and self-employment income you and your partner earn while an RDP; and
3. income from real estate treated as community property under state laws where the property is located.

Separate Property and Separate Income - General Rules

In general, separate property can come from several sources, and it is possible for an RDP to acquire separate property AFTER the date of RDP registration.

Separate **property** will generally include

1. all assets owned separately **before** registration as a domestic partnership or January 1, 2007, whichever date is later;
2. assets received as a gift (before and after registration);
3. assets received as an inheritance (before and after registration);
4. assets acquired with your separate property (before and after registration);

5. property that you and your partner agree to convert from community to separate property (see following section on gift taxes); and

6. money earned while domiciled in a noncommunity property state.

Separate **income** will generally include

1. income from your separate property (see above).

In addition, you will also need to determine if potentially tax-deductible items are paid from community property or separate property funds to assess the amount deductible by each partner. In some cases, expenses paid from community funds will be deductible to one partner but not the other.

Planning Point:

Separate Means Separate

If you have identified an asset as separate property or receive a gift of separate property during your partnership, this asset should not be commingled with community property assets. Doing so may taint the character of the separate property, and, if the assets are commingled in a way that prohibits their identification as separate property, you may not be able to recover them upon termination of the partnership or use them as separate property for tax planning purposes.

For example, assume you have a joint checking account into which both you and your partner deposit your paychecks (which are community income). Further assume your Aunt gave you $5,000 - a gift that is separate property to you - and you deposit the $5,000 into the joint checking account. Throughout the year, you and your partner cover your daily living expenses from the joint account. At times the balance in the account is as low as $100. At the end of the year, the account has accumulated $12,000. What portion of the account is yours? Do you and your partner each own one-half of it -$6,000 each assuming that the SP was spent and what remains is 100% CP? Or, are you entitled to $8,500- your $5,000 of separate property plus one-half of the remainder which is community property ($5,000 SP + 1/2 x ($12,000 - $5,000 SP)) - and your partner to $3,500 (1/2 ($12,000 - $5,000))? Finally, if the SP was spent, what was it spent on? If you have commingled your property, it is advisable to seek legal assistance to determine the character of your assets.

CP/SP Worksheet Example

As noted above, a CP/SP Worksheet should be completed at the time of registration and then updated at least annually. Completion of the CP/SP worksheet will then be used to determine the proper reporting for many items in the tax return.

Let's assume the following facts about Jezebel and Rita. Jezebel and Rita registered as domestic partners in California on July 1, 2009. On July 1, 2009, Jezebel owned a home with a value of $450,000 and a mortgage of $300,000. In addition, Jezebel had a Range Rover worth $5,000, a Wells Fargo checking account with $2,000 in it and 2 stock holdings - 100 shares of White Co. with a value of $15,000 and 50 shares of Black Co. with a value of $3,000. On July 1, 2009, Rita had $500 in her interest bearing checking account at Bank of America and no other assets. After registration, Jezebel and Rita opened a joint checking account at Morgan Stanley into which they deposited their paychecks and paid all of their household bills. They also acquired an additional 60 shares of Black Co. and 20 shares of Red Co. and paid for these shares from their Morgan Stanley account. In addition, Jezebel sold 10 shares of her White Co. and purchased 15 shares of Yellow Co. At December 31, 2010, Jezebel and Rita would complete their CP/SP worksheet in anticipation of preparing their tax return as follows:

CP/SP Worksheet

Use this worksheet to document all of your property and its CP/SP character

Partner 1 =	Jezebel
Partner 2 =	Rita
Date of Registration as Washington SRDPs	7/1/09
Date of Worksheet	12/31/10

List/Description of Property	CP	SP Ptr 1	SP Ptr 2	Notes
Wells Fargo Checking		X		Jez's pre-RDP account
Bank of America Checking			X	Rita's pre-RDP account
Morgan Stanley Checking	X			Our community account
90 shares White Co.		X		See note below
50 shares of Black Co.		X		
60 shares of Black Co.	X			Bought w/ CP funds
20 shares of Red Co.	X			Bought w/ CP funds
15 shares of Yellow Co.		X		See note below
Home & Mortgage		X		

Additional Notes:

Jez sold 10 of her White Co. shares that were her SP and purchased 15 shares of Yellow Co.

Note that Jezebel and Rita did not report their income from these investments on this schedule. Completing this worksheet is just the first step to preparing the returns. In order to properly report CP and SP income, it is necessary to start with a complete inventory of each asset and its CP/SP character. Once the schedule is completed, the couple will simply update it each year with any relevant changes. We will return to this example in later sections of the Guide to illustrate how this worksheet is used to help properly characterize income and deductions for use in preparing your tax returns.

Pre- and Post-Partnership Agreements (PPAs)

California residents may choose to enter into a pre-partnership agreement or a post-partnership agreement (PPAs), which will allow them control how their property will be divided if they terminate their partnership or one of them dies. These agreements can also impact how income is reported for Federal tax purposes, so, if you have entered into an agreement, you must consider its terms when filing your tax return. For these agreements to be enforced by the court, there must be full-disclosure between the couple with respect to sources of income, property and debts. In addition, the couple must act in accordance with the agreement during the partnership.

In general, if you are considering entering into a pre- or post-partnership agreement, both you and your partner should hire independent legal counsel. Hiring an attorney will help you to be fully informed of your rights and insure that you have a carefully written document that will be enforced by the courts.

The Basics of Gift Taxation

The United States has two different tax systems - an income tax system that applies to the annual earnings of individuals and a gift and estate tax system that relates to the lifetime transfer of wealth. Most people have at least a basic understanding of the income tax system, but the Gift and Estate tax system is not widely understood. Normally, this vague understanding of the gift and estate tax system is not a problem because individuals are allowed certain annual and lifetime exclusions that cover most wealth transfers; but, since RDPs/SSMCs are not considered married for purposes of either system, there can be situations in which a simple transaction between partners will trigger a taxable transfer that requires filing a gift tax return. This Guide briefly summarizes the rules as they relate to gifts made during your lifetime. Rules with respect to transfers at death are beyond the scope of this discussion. Before entering any transaction in which rights or property are transferred between partners, you should consult with an attorney qualified to advise you in gift and estate taxation.

Gifts and the Annual Exclusion

With limited exceptions, any time you give someone cash or property without an expectation of payment, you have made a gift. For instance, if you give your brother $5,000, you have made a gift; if you give your sister a bicycle you purchased for $500, you have made a gift; if you give your neighbors $2,000 to pay their rent, you have made a gift.

In 2010, individuals are allowed to make gifts during the year up to $13,000 per donee without filing a gift tax return. That means you can give $13,000 to your brother, $13,000 to your sister, and $13,000 to your neighbor and you don't have to file a gift tax return even though your total gifts were $39,000 ($13,000 + $13,000 + $13,000). If, on the other hand, you give $39,000 to your brother, you do have to file a gift tax return because you have exceeded the $13,000 per donee annual exclusion.

RDPs/SSMCs and the Gift Tax System

Since community property statutes apply to California RDP/SSMCs, situations can occur in which a gift made by one partner to a third party results in both partners being required to file gift tax returns. In addition, some transfers between RDPs/SSMCs may be subject to the gift tax. Examples for two of these situations will be discussed in the following paragraphs. As stated before, this Guide is not a comprehensive review of gift and estate taxes and cannot be used as a substitute for consultation with an attorney on these types of matters. The purpose of this Guide is to raise your awareness of the issues.

RDP/SSMC Gift Example 1 - Gifts from CP versus SP

Gifts made by one California RDPs/SSMCs can result in a gift being made by both partners since a gift of community property is considered made one-half by each partner. The application of how community property rules can result in gifts can be illustrated by a series of simple examples.

Assume that Bartok and Hobart are RDPs domiciled in California. Bartok likes to make gifts and can make the gifts either from SP or CP property. The Table below summarizes Bartok and Hobart's responsibility for filing gift tax returns in a number of different gifting situations. When Bartok makes gifts from SP (first three rows of the table) Hobart has no responsibility to file gift tax returns and Bartok only has to file gift tax returns when his gift to a single donee exceeds $13,000 (highlighted cells). However, when Bartok makes a gift from CP (last three rows of the table) the gift is considered made one-half by Bartok and one-half by Hobart. Bartok can make gifts up to $26,000 to a single donee from CP, and the gift is considered $13,000 from Bartok and $13,000 from Hobart. In this situation, since the reportable gift is not greater than $13,000, neither Bartok nor Hobart is required to file a gift tax return. However, if Bartok makes a gift greater than $26,000 from CP, both Bartok and Hobart are required to file gift tax returns reporting a $20,000 gift to the donee (bottom row).

| | Gift | | Assumed Share of Gift | |
Donor	Amount	SP or CP	Bartok	Hobart
Bartok	$12,000	SP	$12,000	$0
Bartok	$26,000	SP	$26,000	$0
Bartok	$40,000	SP	$40,000	$0
Bartok	$12,000	CP	$6,000	$6,000
Bartok	$26,000	CP	$13,000	$13,000
Bartok	$40,000	CP	$20,000	$20,000

RDP Gift Example 2 - Exchange for less than Fair Market Value (FMV)

A second common gifting situation that can occur, particularly with RDPs/SSMCs, is the transfer of real property between the partners.

Transfer of Property to your Partner

Let's assume you own a home that you purchased for $100,000 (your basis) with a current market value of $250,000 prior to becoming an RDP. When you become an RDP, you might decide to put your partner on title of your home so that you both have a 50% interest in the property. If you do this, you will have made a $125,000 gift to your partner (50% of the $250,000 market value) and you will need to file a Gift Tax Return to report this transaction even if you do not owe tax.

Transfer of Property subject to a Mortgage to your Partner

Take the same situation as above but assume that the $250,000 home is subject to a $150,000 mortgage and your partner also becomes liable for his or her share of the mortgage upon transfer. In this case the net value of the transfer is $50,000 (50% x ($250,000 - $150,000)), and, therefore, you might believe there is a gift of $50,000. However, this analysis is incorrect.

The correct analysis in this situation is that you have a partial gift equal to 50% of the equity - or $50,000 - and a partial sale of the property which, depending on the donor's basis in the property, may also result in a taxable gain to the transferor. If you have this situation currently or in the past, you should consult legal counsel and/or a tax advisor. You may need to file some past due gift and/or income tax returns to properly report the transactions.

Gifts and the Unified Credit

Although you may be required to file gift tax returns, it is unlikely you will have to write a check to pay any gift tax due to the Unified Credit. Currently, the unified credit can be used to offset the tax on cumulative lifetime taxable gifts up to $5,000,000. Basically, when you make gifts greater than $13,000 to a donee, you report the taxable gift on your gift tax return, calculate the gift tax and then "pay" any tax due with the unified credit. Even though no cash payment is due, you **must** file a gift tax return to report the taxable gifts and the use of the unified credit. The amount being sheltered by the unified credit can change significantly with changes in tax legislation so, it is important to consult with a qualified estate and gift tax attorney if you plan to make any large transfers.

Planning Point:

Consistent Plan of Lifetime Transfers

Many RDPs find themselves in situations where one partner has significantly greater pre-RDP assets than the other partner. Rather than making one large transfer and using part of your lifetime unified credit, consider entering into a plan of small annual transfers that are less than or equal to the annual maximum gift tax exclusion. At the current annual exclusion amount, you could transfer $130,000 in 10 years.

Filing Status

In general, both partners will file separate US tax returns using the Single filing status (S). However, the Head of household filing status (HOH) has more favorable tax rates than the single filing status, and it can be beneficial for the couple to arrange their affairs so that one of the partners qualifies as HOH.

In the introduction we showed that recognition of community property rights could result in significantly reduced combined tax liabilities for couples with one partner who earns less than the other. RDPs/SSMCs can also benefit from qualifying for HOH status, and this tax savings is not dependent on a disparity in income. For example, if one member of a couple has taxable income of $100,000 (reporting income and deductions in accordance with CCA 201021050), his or her 2010 tax using the Single filing status would be $21,709 whereas the tax liability using the HOH filing status would be $19,847 - an annual tax savings of $1,862.

Qualifying for Head-of-Household Filing Status

To qualify as HOH, an RDP/SSMC filer must meet the following criteria:

1. The taxpayer is not married at the end of the year.

   This reference to marriage means marriage as recognized by US tax law. Under DOMA, a same-sex married couple is not considered married. Therefore, RDPs will not be considered married for this rule under current tax law.

2. The taxpayer pays more than one-half of the cost of keeping up the home.

3. The taxpayer is a US citizen or resident during the entire year.

4. The home was the principal residence for more than one-half of the year for a qualifying relative.

Qualifying relatives include

   qualifying single child;

   dependent married child;

   qualifying dependent relative; or

   dependent parent - even if the parent did not live in the taxpayer's home as long as the taxpayer provides more than one-half of the parent's support.

The rules for determining whether an individual meets the requirements for a qualifying relative are complex, and a complete discussion of these rules is beyond the scope of the Guide. If you believe you may qualify under one of the more complicated rules, consult a tax adviser and/or IRS Pub 17 to determine whether you qualify for HOH status.

Planning Point

Meeting the Support Requirement for HOH Status

To qualify for HOH status you or your partner must provide over one-half support for a qualifying dependent. To do this, the partner planning to claim HOH status should plan to pay at least one household bill per year from separate property and all the rest from community property. One way to remember to do this is for the HOH partner to make it a practice to pay the January utility bills each year from cash received as a holiday gift or from other separate property.

Remember, only one SRDP can claim HOH - you both can't provide over one-half support for the same qualifying dependent, so make sure to coordinate your efforts!

Wages & Withholding Taxes

HOW MUCH to Report on Your Tax Returns

Splitting Wages and Withholding - Simple Case

Income from wages is community property in California. What this means for you as an RDP is that one-half of your wages and withheld taxes are actually attributed to your partner and one-half of his or her wages and withheld taxes are attributed to you. This makes reporting income on your tax return a little more complicated.

Let's look at how the items reported on a W-2 would be recorded on your tax return. Following are the actual amounts reported on Bartok and Hobart's Forms W-2 in 2010.

Item Reported	Bartok	Hobart	Total
Wages	$200,000	$80,000	$280,000
Federal Tax Withholding	$60,000	$15,000	$75,000

If the wages had been earned before Bartok and Hobart became RDPs, Bartok would have reported his wages of $200,000 on line 1 of Form 1040 and reported $60,000 of federal withholding on line 61 on page 2 of the return. Similarly, Hobart would have reported his wages of $80,000 on line 1 and $15,000 of federal withholding on line 61 of his tax return.

However, since this example is set in 2010 and Bartok and Hobart are RDPs, CCA 201021050 requires the wages to be split and reported in accordance with California's State community property laws. The amount to be reported is therefore calculated as follows:

Wages Reported	Bartok's CP Share	Hobart's CP Share	Total
Bartok's Wages	$100,000	$100,000	$200,000
Hobart's Wages	40,000	40,000	80,000
Total Reported on TR	$140,000	$140,000	$280,000

In addition, the withholding (and any other items on Form W-2 that are reported in the US tax return) must be split and reported as follows:

Withholding Reported	Bartok's CP Share	Hobart's CP Share	Total
Bartok's Withholding	$30,000	$30,000	$60,000
Hobart's Withholding	7,500	7,500	15,000
Total Reported on TR	$37,500	$37,500	$75,000

How to report the wages and withholding on your tax returns is discussed in more detail in later in the Guide.

Splitting Wages and Withholding - Year of Registration as RDP

If you register as a domestic partner after the start of the tax year and do not enter into a PPA, your wages prior to the date of registration will be separate property, reported 100% on your tax return, and wages after the date of registration will be community property, split between you and your partner. Let's assume that Jezebel and Rita became registered domestic partners on June 30th of the 2010 tax year. Jezebel's pay statement for June 28th (the closest pay date prior to the date of their registration) shows Jezebel's year-to-date (YTD) wages to be $90,000 and her total wages for 2010 reported on her form W-2 are $200,000. Rita's pay statement for June 28th shows her YTD wages to be $30,000 and her total wages for 2010 reported on her form W-2 are $80,000. As shown in the following table, Jezebel's taxable income of $170,000 includes wages from three sources -

$90,000 which is 100% of her pre-RDP wages; plus

$55,000 which is one-half of her post-RDP wages (50% x $110,000); plus

$25,000, which is one-half of Rita's post-RDP wages (50% x $50,000)

Wages Reported	Jezebel Reports	Rita Reports	Total
Pre-SRDP Wages - Jezebel	$90,000	$0	$90,000
Post-SRDP Wages - Jezebel	55,000	55,000	110,000
Pre-SRDP Wages - Rita	0	30,000	30,000
Post-SRDP Wages - Rita	25,000	25,000	50,000
Total Reported	$170,000	$110,000	$280,000

Rita's wages and withholding (and any other relevant items reported on Form W-2) will be calculated in a similar manner using the pay statement immediately before the partners registered with the State to determine pre-RDP amounts.

HOW TO Report on Your Tax Returns

There is a difference between determining HOW MUCH to report on your tax returns and HOW TO report these amounts on your tax returns. In the Simple Case for Bartok and Hobart presented above we determined HOW MUCH to report. In this scenario we determined that Bartok should report $140,000 of wages and $37,500 of federal withholding and Hobart should report $140,000 of wages and $37,500 of federal withholding. However, due to the IRS matching program, Bartok and Hobart can't just report the line item amounts shown in the above example on their respective tax returns because these amounts will not agree with the W-2 information that was provided to the IRS by their employer.

To minimize the matching problem RDPs, will need to report their wages so that line 1 of their tax returns agrees with the amount reported on their Form W-2. Then, to arrive at the "correct" amount of income to be reported on their tax return in accordance with the community income splitting rules, they will report either a positive or negative "RDP adjustment" on the other income line (line 21) of their tax return as illustrated below.

HOW TO Report Wages - Bartok's Tax Return

Income	7	Wages, salaries, tips, etc. Attach Form(s) W-2	7	200,000
	8a	Taxable interest. Attach Schedule B if required	8a	
	b	Tax-exempt interest. Do not include on line 8a . . . 8b		
Attach Form(s) W-2 here. Also attach Forms W-2G and 1099-R if tax was withheld.	9a	Ordinary dividends. Attach Schedule B if required	9a	
	b	Qualified dividends 9b		
	10	Taxable refunds, credits, or offsets of state and local income taxes	10	
	11	Alimony received	11	
	12	Business income or (loss). Attach Schedule C or C-EZ	12	
If you did not get a W-2, see page 20.	13	Capital gain or (loss). Attach Schedule D if required. If not required, check here □	13	
	14	Other gains or (losses). Attach Form 4797	14	
	15a	IRA distributions . 15a b Taxable amount . . .	15b	
	16a	Pensions and annuities 16a b Taxable amount . . .	16b	
	17	Rental real estate, royalties, partnerships, S corporations, trusts, etc. Attach Schedule E	17	
Enclose, but do not attach, any payment. Also, please use Form 1040-V.	18	Farm income or (loss). Attach Schedule F	18	
	19	Unemployment compensation	19	
	20a	Social security benefits 20a b Taxable amount . . .	20b	
	21	Other income. List type and amount RDP Adjustment	21	(60,000)
	22	Combine the amounts in the far right column for lines 7 through 21. This is your total income	22	140,000

HOW TO Report Wages - Hobart's Tax Return

Income	7	Wages, salaries, tips, etc. Attach Form(s) W-2	7	100,000
	8a	Taxable interest. Attach Schedule B if required	8a	
	b	Tax-exempt interest. Do not include on line 8a . . . 8b		
Attach Form(s) W-2 here. Also attach Forms W-2G and 1099-R if tax was withheld.	9a	Ordinary dividends. Attach Schedule B if required	9a	
	b	Qualified dividends 9b		
	10	Taxable refunds, credits, or offsets of state and local income taxes	10	
	11	Alimony received	11	
	12	Business income or (loss). Attach Schedule C or C-EZ	12	
If you did not get a W-2, see page 20.	13	Capital gain or (loss). Attach Schedule D if required. If not required, check here □	13	
	14	Other gains or (losses). Attach Form 4797	14	
	15a	IRA distributions . 15a b Taxable amount . . .	15b	
	16a	Pensions and annuities 16a b Taxable amount . . .	16b	
	17	Rental real estate, royalties, partnerships, S corporations, trusts, etc. Attach Schedule E	17	
Enclose, but do not attach, any payment. Also, please use Form 1040-V.	18	Farm income or (loss). Attach Schedule F	18	
	19	Unemployment compensation	19	
	20a	Social security benefits 20a b Taxable amount . . .	20b	
	21	Other income. List type and amount RDP Adjustment	21	60,000
	22	Combine the amounts in the far right column for lines 7 through 21. This is your total income	22	140,000

As illustrated in the figures above, Bartok would report $200,000 of wages on line 1 of his tax return and a negative $60,000 as an RDP Adjustment on line 21 of his Form 1040 as shown. Likewise, Hobart would report $80,000 of wages on line 1 of his tax return and a positive $60,000 as an RDP Adjustment on line 21 of his Form 1040.

In addition to reporting their wages in this manner on page 1 of their tax return, RDPs must also attach a "Publication 555" worksheet to their returns. An example of this worksheet is included in Appendix D. The worksheet should show the allocation of all income and deduction between the two RDPs. Taxpayers should also included a worksheet that shows the allocation of withholding between the two RDPs. An example of this withholding worksheet is also included in Appendix D. Further instructions and a list of attachments to include with your returns is included in the section titled "Filing Your Tax Returns with the IRS."

Interest & Dividends

After completing the section on wages, you may be thinking, "This is pretty easy. We just take our income and divide by two." Unfortunately, it is not that easy. For each source of income and deduction, there is usually some twist or peculiarity to the tax law that prevents RDPs/SSMCs from simply dividing everything by two. Wages are a special case because they are earned based on your current efforts. If you are an RDP at the time you earn the wages, the wages are community income and therefore shared by you and your partner unless you have a PPA or meet some other exception.

Unlike wages, interest and dividends are earned on assets (cash, stock, CDs, etc.) that you and your partner acquired sometime in the past. The character of that income - SP or CP - depends on whether the asset was acquired with SP or CP funds. If an asset was acquired with SP funds, the earnings on that asset will be SP. If an asset was acquired with CP funds, the earnings on that asset will be CP. This distinction is one reason why it is important for you to complete the CP/SP worksheet prior to starting the tax return preparation process.

In January or early February of each year you will receive Form 1099s reporting the amount of interest and dividends you earned on invested funds during the previous year. The investments on which you earn the interest and dividends should already be listed on your CP/SP Worksheet and identified as CP or SP property. Once both you and your partner have completed the CP/SP worksheet and have the current year 1099s, you are ready to complete this portion of your tax return.

Preparing the interest and dividend portion of your tax return is a two-step process. The first step is to determine HOW MUCH each partner is going to report. Once you know how much to report, you must then determine exactly HOW TO report those amounts. We will use Jezebel and Rita's CP/SP example to illustrate this process in the following paragraphs.

HOW MUCH to Report on Your Tax Returns

In early 2011 Jezebel and Rita received Forms 1099 reporting interest or dividends taxable in 2010:

Income Source	Reported SSN	2010 Interest $'s	2010 Dividends $'s	CP/SP
Wells Fargo	Jez	$40	$0	SP Jez
Bank of America	Rita	10	0	SP Rita
Morgan Stanley	Jez	80	0	CP
White Co Shares	Jez	0	800	SP Jez
Black Co Shares	Jez	0	75	SP Jez
Black Co Shares	Jez	0	90	CP
Red Co Shares	Rita	0	60	CP
Yellow Co Shares	Jez	0	100	SP Jez
Total		$130	$1,125	

In the first step, we use the CP/SP worksheet previously completed by Jezebel and Rita to determine how much interest and dividend income is reported on their tax returns.

CP/SP Worksheet

Use this worksheet to document all of your property and its CP/SP character

Partner 1 =   Jezebel
Partner 2 =   Rita
Date of Registration as Washington SRDPs   7/1/09
Date of Worksheet   12/31/10

List/Description of Property	CP	SP Ptr 1	SP Ptr 2	Notes
Wells Fargo Checking		X		Jez's pre-RDP account
Bank of America Checking			X	Rita's pre-RDP account
Morgan Stanley Checking	X			Our community account
90 shares White Co.		X		See note below
50 shares of Black Co.		X		
60 shares of Black Co.	X			Bought w/ CP funds
20 shares of Red Co.	X			Bought w/ CP funds
15 shares of Yellow Co.		X		See note below
Home & Mortgage		X		

Additional Notes:

Jez sold 10 of her White Co. shares that were her SP and purchased 15 shares of Yellow Co.

Using a notebook or electronic spreadsheet, Jezebel and Rita would create the following worksheet to calculate the amount of interest and dividends to report in their tax returns.

Income Source	Jezebel		Rita	
	Interest	Dividends	Interest	Dividends
Wells Fargo	$40	$0	$0	$0
Bank of America	0	0	10	0
Morgan Stanley	40	0	40	0
White Co Shares	0	800	0	0
Black Co Shares	0	75	0	0
Black Co Shares	0	45	0	45
Red Co Shares	0	30	0	30
Yellow Co Shares	0	100	0	0
Total	$80	$1,050	$50	$75

Income from SP, like Jezebel's ownership of her Wells Fargo account, is listed 100% in the column of the owner. Income that is CP, like the Morgan Stanley account is split between the two owners even though is it reported under Jezebel's social security number (SSN). Once completed, this worksheet tells you HOW MUCH will be reported on each RDPs tax return in total.

Planning Point

Be Consistent in Reporting Information from Forms 1099

Form 1099s often include much more tax reporting information than the examples shown above. For instance, information on qualified dividends, foreign tax credits, municipal bond interest, US interest and interest on special activity bonds may be reported as part of your tax information. All of this information is relevant to completing your tax return, and, if the asset generating this information is CP, the appropriate share must be reported on each partner's return. Failure to split all of the information reported on the Form 1099 is a common error on RDP returns.

HOW TO Report on Your Tax Returns

As with wages and withholding, there is a difference between determining HOW MUCH interest and dividends to report on your tax returns and HOW TO report these amounts on your tax returns. In the previous section we determined HOW MUCH to report. Jezebel should report $80 of interest and $1,050 of dividends. Rita should report $50 of interest and $75 of dividends. However, due to the IRS matching program, you shouldn't just report the amounts as shown in the HOW MUCH section above. As shown in the following table, one way to minimize the matching problem is to report the full amount of any interest or dividends that were reported to your SSN and then show a positive or negative "RDP Adjustment" to arrive at the correct amount to report based on the income splitting rules. Following is an example of how Jezebel and Rita would actually report the interest income on their tax returns.

Income Source	Jezebel's Tax Return	Rita's Tax Return
Wells Fargo	$40	$0
Bank of America	0	10
Morgan Stanley	80	0
RDP Adjustment	(40)	40
Total Interest	$80	$50

Both Jezebel and Rita would report 100% of the amounts reported under their respective SSN's, and then they would add one more reporting line titled "RDP Adjustment" to show the amount of additional or reduced income that should be reported due to the income splitting rules. Note that the total interest reported is always the same, it is just the breakout between the two partners' tax returns that changes.

On Schedule B (the form where taxpayers report their income from interest and dividends) Jezebel would report $40 of interest income from Wells Fargo and $80 of interest income from Morgan Stanley. Then, she would also include an additional line called "RDP Adjustment" and report a negative $40 to come to a total interest income of $80. Rita would report the $10 of interest on her SP from Bank of American and a positive $40 RDP Adjustment to show her share of the Morgan Stanley interest reported under Jezebel's SSN.

Following is an example of how Jezebel and Rita would actually report the dividend income on their tax returns.

Income Source	Jezebel's Tax Return	Rita's Tax Return
White Co Shares	$800	$0
Black Co Shares	75	0
Black Co Shares	90	0
Red Co Shares	0	60
Yellow Co Shares	100	0
RDP Adjustment	(15)	15
Total Dividends	$1,050	$75

Self-Employment Income & Estimated Payments

While the question of how to report wages for RDP/SSMC couples is fairly well settled, the question of how to report self-employment (SE) income is not. RDP/SSMC taxpayers face a choice between two alternative methods of reporting SE income which can have an impact on 1) the amount of SE tax paid, 2) the social security credits earned by a taxpayer - which can affect future social security benefits, and 3) contributions to a taxpayer's self-employed retirement plans.

HOW MUCH to Report

For purposes of illustrating this topic, let's assume that Bartok and Hobart are a California RDP couple in 2010. Bartok works full-time for a company and earns wages of $200,000. Hobart works full-time in his own business and earns $120,000 of SE income. Bartok does not work in Hobart's business.

Since they are RDPs, Bartok and Hobart will each report $160,000 of income on their return respective tax returns Each partner will report $100,000 of Bartok's wages and $60,000 of Hobart's SE income.

The amount of income reported is the same under both alternatives, but HOW TO report the amount of income allocated to each partner that is subject to SE tax is different as shown in the following paragraphs. Currently, Alternative 2 is the method suggested by the IRS.

HOW TO Report SE Income

Alternative 1 – Allocated SE Income Does Not Retain Character

The first alternative splits SE income between the RDPs in a manner that is consistent with how wages are treated. Bartok will report 100% of his wage income on line 1 of Form 1040, and Hobart will report 100% of his SE Income on line 12 of Form 1040. Both Bartok and Hobart will then report an RDP adjustment on line 21 of Form 1040 to reflect splitting of their community property income.

	Alternative 1	
As Reported on Tax Return	Bartok	Hobart
Wages	$200,000	$0
SE Income	0	120,000
RDP Adjustment:		
Bartok's Wages	(100,000)	100,000
Hobart's SE Income	60,000	(60,000)
Total Income	$160,000	$160,000

Regular Tax	$35,891	$33,587
SE Tax	0	16,457
Total Tax	$35,891	$50,044

As shown above, Bartok's line 21 RDP adjustment is a net negative adjustment of $40,000 - a negative adjustment of $100,000 to reflect the allocation of $100,000 of Bartok's wages to Hobart and a positive $60,000 to reflect the allocation of $60,000 of Hobart's SE income to Bartok. Hobart's line 21 adjustment is a net positive adjustment of $40,000 reflecting a positive allocation of $100,000 of Bartok's wages to Hobart and a negative adjustment of $60,000 of Hobart's SE income to Bartok.

The significance of this method of reporting is that Hobart will pay 100% of the SE taxes on his SE income, receiving full credit for these earnings toward his future social security retirement. The total taxes (regular and SE) reported under this alternative are $85,935.

Alternative 2 – Allocated SE Income Does Retain Character

The second alternative splits SE income between the RDPs as if both partners have earned one-half of the SE income. Bartok will still report 100% of his wage income on line 1 of Form 1040, but he will also report one-half of the SE income on line 12 of Form 1040 rather than as an RDP adjustment on line 21. Hobart will report one-half of his total SE Income on line 12 of Form 1040. Since the SE income split has been reported directly on line 12, the RDP adjustment on line 21 will only include the adjustment to allocate one-half of Bartok's wages.

As Reported on Tax Return	Alternative 2	
	Bartok	Hobart
Wages	$200,000	$0
SE Income	60,000	60,000
RDP Adjustment:		
Bartok's Wages	(100,000)	100,000
Hobart's SE Income	0	0
Total Income	$160,000	$160,000

Regular Tax	$35,666	$34,704
SE Tax	1,607	8,478
Total Tax	$37,273	$43,182

The significance of this method of reporting is that Bartok and Hobart will each calculate SE taxes on 50% of the total SE income and receive credit for these earnings toward their future social security retirement. The total taxes (regular and SE) reported under this alternative are $80,455. The reduction in overall taxes between the two methods is due to the fact that Bartok is already paying the maximum social security tax on his wages, and, therefore, Bartok is paying only the Medicare tax on the SE income.

Although Alternative 2 would appear to save taxes, there is a possible cost to these savings. First, the amount Hobart can contribute to a self-employed retirement plan is reduced under this method. The maximum SEP-IRA for Hobart with $120,000 SE income is $22,354 whereas the maximum SEP-IRA for Hobart with $60,000 of SE income is $11,152. In addition, since the SEP-IRA is deductible for income tax purposes, the additional deduction associated with the larger SEP-IRA contribution would save Hobart over $4,200.

Both Partners Active in SE Business

If both partners are active in the SE business, then the partners report SE income on both returns consistent with Alternative 2.

Estimated Payments are not Allocated Between Partners

In general, taxpayers are required to pay taxes on income as it is earned. There are two ways to pay your taxes throughout the year - through withholding on wages and through quarterly estimated tax payments. As we discussed in the section on wages, withholding is allocated between RDPs in a manner consistent with the allocation of wages. However, estimated tax payments, which are usually made by self-employed persons, *are not* allocated between RDPs even if the SE income is allocated. When taxpayers make an estimated payment, they send the payment with a voucher that has their SSN on it, and the IRS credits the payment to the specific taxpayer's account. The estimated payments will be reported on the tax return of the person under whose SSN the payment was made. Thus, it is important that both RDPs plan ahead and make separate estimated payments under their separate SSNs when there is shared SE income.

As an example, assume that $25,000 was withheld on Bartok's wages, and Hobart made estimated tax payments during the year of $50,000. Bartok's tax return would show $12,500 as a credit against any taxes owed (one-half of the $25,000 withheld from his wages) and Hobart would show $62,500 as a credit against taxes (one half of the $25,000 withheld on Bartok's wages plus 100% of the estimated tax payments of $50,000 made by Hobart). Since the estimated tax payments are allocated 100% to Hobart - the person who made the payment - Bartok would be significantly underpaid, and Hobart would be overpaid. Bartok's underpayment could result in significant penalties.

Capital Gains & Losses

Gain and Loss from Stock and Other Assets

Determining the tax treatment of gains and losses from stock and other assets is similar to determining the treatment of interest and dividends. Income allocation of the gain or loss on the sale of these assets will depend on whether the assets are SP or CP. If the asset is SP, the gain/loss on the sale is SP. If the asset is CP, the gain/loss on the sale is CP and should be split between your and your partner's returns.

Similar to interest and dividends, you should tackle gains and losses in two pieces - first determine HOW MUCH is to be reported on each return, then determine HOW TO report the items on the returns to reduce matching notices.

HOW MUCH to Report on Your Tax Returns

Returning to the example of Jezebel and Rita, let's assume that they had sold 10 shares of White stock

How Much to Report in Total

Description	Date Acquired	Date Sold	Sales Proceeds	Cost	Gain (Loss)
10 Shares White	15-Feb-00	1-Jun-10	$1,600	$400	$1,200
10 Shares Red	23-Aug-08	1-Jun-10	800	600	200
Total			$2,400	$1,000	$1,400

and 10 shares of Red stock in 2010 with gain calculated as follows:

If Jezebel and Rita were able to file a joint return, the total gain recorded by them on their return would be $1,400 - regardless of whether the property was CP or SP. However, from the previous example, we know that the 10 shares of White stock were Jezebel's SP property, and the 10 shares of Red stock were CP. The sale of the White shares are reported by the broker on Form 1099B using Jezebel's SSN. The sales of the Red shares are reported by the broker on Form 1099B using Rita's SSN. Although the total gain recognized by the two RDPs will be $1,400, HOW TO report it on their tax returns is covered in the following section.

HOW TO Report on Your Tax Returns

Since the White shares are Jezebel's separate property, she will report 100% of the $1,200 gain on her tax return. In addition, since the Red shares are CP, Jezebel will report one-half of the gain on the sale of those shares (50% of $200 gain) on her tax return for a total gain from sale of stock of $1,300.

How to Report - Jezebel's Tax Return

Description	Date Acquired	Date Sold	Sales Proceeds	Cost	Gain (Loss)
10 Shares White	15-Feb-00	1-Jun-10	$1,600	$400	$1,200
RDP Adj - Red Shares				(100)	100
Total			$1,600	$300	$1,300

It is important to note a couple of things about how the gain is reported on Jezebel's tax return. Brokers report gross proceeds from the sale of stocks to the IRS, and the IRS uses this information in its computer-matching program. If the gross proceeds reported on your tax return do not equal or exceed the amount of gross proceeds reported to the IRS by your broker, you will probably receive a matching notice letter from the IRS asking you to explain the difference. To avoid these notices, you should:

1. make sure that gross proceeds on your tax return equal or exceed gross proceeds reported to you on your Forms 1099B and
2. adjust your schedule to reflect all 'RDP Adjustments' only through the COST column of Schedule D - the form on which you report Gains and Losses on your tax return.

Since Jezebel needs to report $100 of the gain from the sale of Red stock, we will input $0 in the Sales proceeds column and a negative $100 in the cost column (less cost means more gain), which results in a positive $100 in the gain column. This results in a total gain of $1,300 being reported on Jezebel's tax return.

Although the Red Shares are CP property, they were reported under Rita's SSN by the broker, so the total gain will be reported on Rita's return and then reduced by one-half to reflect the portion reported on Jezebel's tax return.

To reflect the RDP Adjustment on Rita's return, we report 0 in proceeds and $100 in the cost column (increased cost means less gain), which results in a negative $100 in the gain (loss) column.

How to Report - Rita's Tax Return

Description	Date Acquired	Date Sold	Sales Proceeds	Cost	Gain (Loss)
10 Shares Red	23-Aug-08	1-Jun-10	$800	$600	$200
RDP Adj - Red Shares				100	(100)
Total			$800	$700	$100

If you are splitting a loss, you simply reverse the entry in the cost column. If there had been a $300 loss reported on Rita's return that was CP, the adjustment on Rita's return (to reduce the loss by one-half) would be a negative $150 in cost and the adjustment on Jezebel's return (to report one-half of the loss) would be a positive $150 in the cost column.

After completing both partners' returns, you should double check your adjustments by adding together the total gain/loss reported on each return and verifying that it equals the amount you originally calculated to be the total gain/loss. For instance, the total gain to be reported by Jezebel and Rita was $1,400, and our examples add to this amount - $1,300 on Jezebel's tax return and $100 on Rita's tax return.

Capital Loss Carryforwards

One reporting item individuals find confusing but that is, in fact, quite straightforward is how to handle capital loss carryforwards. When capital losses exceed capital gains, you are allowed to carry the excess loss forward to future tax returns. If the loss was generated before you became an RDP, then the loss carryforward is SP, and you should report it on your tax return only - you should not split it with your RDP. When you file your 2010 return, you will split any current year losses on CP property on the two tax returns. If the current year allocated losses combined with current year allocated gains and prior year capital loss carryforwards exceed $3,000 loss (the maximum amount of net capital loss you can deduct on your 2010 tax return), then you will have a capital loss carryforward to 2011. Depending on your RDP's tax situation, he or she may or may not have a capital loss carryforward. For the 2011 tax return, you will use whatever capital loss carryforward was reported on your 2010 tax return, and your RDP will report whatever capital loss carryforward was reported on his or her return. If you amended your 2008 and/or 2009 tax returns, you will use the amount reported on the 2009 *amended* return as your capital loss carryforward for your 2010 tax return.

Stock Options

A full discussion of the taxation of stock options is beyond the scope of this Guide; however, since the income related to these types of transactions can be significant, we will provide a short discussion of the most relevant points. This area is another one where legal counsel is advisable if the amounts under consideration are, or may be, significant.

Accounting for gains on stock options is not as straightforward as accounting for gains on stocks. Stock options can be treated as SP, CP, or a combination of SP and CP depending on when the option is granted and when the option is exercised.

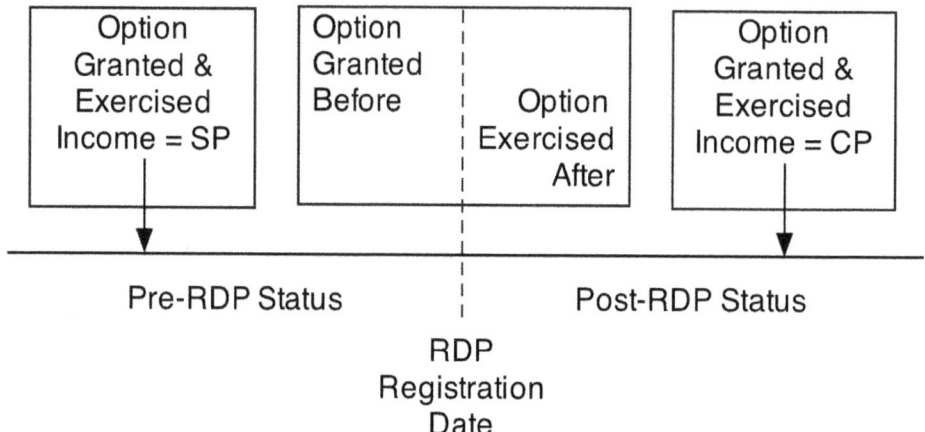

As the illustration above shows, the date on which community property status applies to the RDP couple is critical to determining the tax treatment of stock options. If both the grant and exercise date are before or after this date, the treatment is clear. If the option grant and exercise date are before the date you and your partner enter into community, the property is SP. If the option grant and exercise date are after the date you and your partner enter into community, the property is CP. In general, if the option is granted before you enter community and exercised after you enter community, the portion of the gain that accrues prior to community is SP income, and the portion that accrues after community is CP.

One method for determining the CP/SP status of income from options would be to determine the inherent gain as of the date of RDP registration. Upon exercise of the option, any gain up to the inherent gain at the date of registration could be treated as SP to the earning RDP and gain in excess of the inherent gain would be assumed CP and split between the earning and non-earning RDP since it accrued after the date of registration.

Planning Point

Consider a PPA for Stock Options

PPAs do not have to apply to all assets. RDPs may want to consult an attorney to draft a PPA that applies solely to stock options that have been granted prior to RDP status. If these stock options are identified as SP in a PPA, there will be no ambiguity with respect to taxation upon their eventual exercise. As with any PPA, both RDPs need to be fully aware of both the tax and financial consequences of this action before entering into an agreement that limits their rights with respect to property.

Retirement Income

Taxable retirement income generally comes from one of two sources: pensions that were funded as part of a taxpayer's employment or IRAs (and similar arrangements) that were created and funded by the taxpayer independent of his or her employer. For purposes of RDP community property income splitting, income from these two sources is not treated in the same way. In general, income from IRAs and other similar accounts will be treated as SP, and income from pensions will be allocated between SP and CP based on the earning taxpayer's community property status during the period the funds were earned. Both cases are discussed in more detail in the following paragraphs.

Pensions

According to Pub 555, taxation of pension distributions will depend on when the taxpayer was a participant in the pension plan and when CP rules began to apply to the couple. In addition, the couple must be domiciled in a CP state that recognizes CP rights for the RDP couple. This means that the taxation of the pension will depend not only on registration as an RDP but also on the residence of the RDP couple during the entire period that the pension is being earned.

HOW MUCH to Report on Your Returns

Assume that Bartok and Hobart registered as RDPs in California on September 1, 2009. Bartok began participating in his employer's pension plan on January 1, 1995, and will retire after 20 years in the plan. Bartok and Hobart were domiciled in California during the entire period of their domestic partnership except for two years (2011 and 2012) when they lived in a non-community property state. Bartok's monthly pension upon retirement is $2,000. How will Bartok's pension be split between the two RDP returns in 2015 (Bartok's first full year of retirement)?

Bartok will have been in the plan 20 years and in an RDP with Bartok for 5.5 years. However, because Bartok and Hobart will have lived as RDPs in a non-community property state for 2 of those 5.5 years, only 3.5 years (5.5 years - 2 years) will be used in calculating the allocation of Bartok's pension between the RDPs. Thus, Bartok will recognize $1,650 of the monthly pension distribution ($2,000 x 16.5/20), and Hobart will recognize $350 of the monthly pension distribution ($2,000 x 3.5/20).

HOW TO Report on Your Returns

Pensions are another item that is subject to the federal matching program, so it is important that you report the amounts found on the Forms 1099R that you receive from your plan administrator on your tax return. If you are the partner receiving the pension, report a negative RDP adjustment on Line 21 (Other Income) of your tax return. Your partner should show a positive RDP adjustment for the same amount on Line 21 (Other Income) of their tax return.

> **Planning Point**
>
> **Track Pension Participation**
>
> *People have short memories, and state community property laws change. As part of your annual update of the CP/SP schedule you should also keep a list of where you were living throughout the year. If you move to another state, you should also note what the status of that State's community property laws were during your period of residence with regard to RDPs. Although it is possible for a professional to research State community property laws 20 years after the fact, it is much easier - and less expensive for you - to simply keep contemporaneous records.*

IRAs, SEP-IRAs, SIMPLE IRAs, Roth IRAs and ESAs

According to Pub 555, IRAs (including SEP-IRAs, SIMPLE IRAs and Roth IRAs) as well as Coverdell Educational Savings Accounts (ESAs) are deemed to be separate property for income tax purposes. Distributions from these accounts will be treated as SP and taxable only to the owner of the account even if they were funded with CP. The RDP whose name is on the account is also liable for any penalties and additional tax on early distributions. Since these accounts are treated as SP, there are no allocations to be made between the RDPs.

Other Investments

HOW MUCH to Report - Partnership Income & Loss

The treatment of current year income or loss from a partnership investment will depend on whether the income of the partnership is attributable to the efforts of either of the RDPs. If one of the partners is active in the conduct of the partnership business, the income or loss reported by the partnership will be considered community property income *even if the partnership interest is an SP asset*. This treatment is similar to the treatment of income from wages and self-employment. If the income is due to the current efforts of the partner, then it is community income. However, if the partnership is a passive investment, then the treatment of income or loss reported by the partnership will follow the character of the investment - SP or CP. This treatment is similar to the treatment of other passive investments like savings accounts, CDs, and stock.

Let's assume Bartok owns an SP interest in White Partnership, a passive investment partnership. Hobart owns an SP interest in Hobie Co. Hobart is the CEO of Hobie Co. and is active in the everyday operations of Hobie Co.

Bartok receives a Schedule K-1 from White Partnership reporting the following items:

> Interest Income $200
>
> Short Term Capital Gain $10
>
> Income (loss) from Rental Real Estate ($2,500)

Hobart receives a Schedule K-1 from Hobie Co. reporting the following items:

> Interest Income $300
>
> Short Term Capital Gain $230
>
> Income (loss) from Rental Real Estate ($4,000)

Begin by determining the amount that should be reported in total between the two tax returns:

How Much to Report in Total

Partnership	Reported on Sch K-1		
	Interest Income	Short Term Gain	Rental Real Estate
White Co.	$ 200	$ 10	$ (2,500)
Hobie Co.	300	230	(4,000)
Total	$ 500	$ 240	$ (6,500)

HOW TO Report - Partnership Income & Loss

Since Bartok's interest in White Co. is SP and Bartok is a passive investor in the partnership, 100% of White Co.'s income and loss items are reported on Bartok's return. In addition, Bartok will report one-half of the income and loss items from Hobart's partnership investment in Hobie Co. Although Hobie Co. is an SP asset of Hobart's, Hobart is active in the partnership business and this active participation results in the income from the partnership being reported as CP. Since the Hobie Co. items are reported on a K-1 to Hobart, Bartok's one-half share of the Hobie Co. items will be reported as an RDP Adj. on Bartok's tax return. In this case, the RDP adjustment on Bartok's return will increase interest income by $150 (1/2 of Hobie Co.'s interest reported to Hobart), increase short term capital gain by $115 (1/2 of Hobie Co.'s short term capital gain reported to Hobart) and increase the rental real estate loss by 2,000 (1/2 of Hobie Co.'s rental real estate loss reported to Hobart).

How to Report - Bartok's Return

Partnership	Reported on Sch K-1		
	Interest Income	Short Term Gain	Rental Real Estate
White Co.	$ 200	$ 10	$ (2,500)
RDP Adj.	150	115	(2,000)
Total	$ 350	$ 125	$ (4,500)

Hobart will not report any of the White Co. partnership income because it is Bartok's SP asset *and* a passive investment. The RDP adjustment on Hobart's return will be equal to one-half of the reported

Hobie Co. amounts because, even though Hobie Co. is an SP asset of Hobart, the Hobie Co. investment is an active investment.

How to Report - Hobart's Return

Partnership	Reported on Sch K-1		
	Interest Income	Short Term Gain	Rental Real Estate
Hobie Co.	$ 300	$ 230	$ (4,000)
RDP Adj	(150)	(115)	2,000
Total	$ 150	$ 115	$ (2,000)

As a final check when preparing your tax returns, you should verify that the total amount reported on the two tax returns equals the total amount on your initial worksheet. In this example, the total amount reported for the partnerships on Bartok and Hobart's tax returns after the RDP adjustment is equal to the total reported on the Schedule K-1s.

Rental Income & Loss

Similar to partnership investments, the treatment of current year income or loss from investments in rental real estate will depend on whether the income of the partnership is attributable to the efforts of either of the RDPs. If one of the partners is active in the conduct of the rental real estate investment, the income or loss for the investment will be considered community property income *even if the rental real estate investment is an SP asset*. However, if the rental real estate investment is a passive investment, then the treatment of income or loss for the investment will follow the character of the investment - SP or CP. For further guidance, see the examples for partnership reporting above.

The guidance in Pub 555 is not clear on what level of activity is necessary to require partnership income (or rental real estate income) to be considered community property. The guidance provided in Pub 555 for partnerships is that the income from the partnership will be considered CP if it "is attributable to efforts of either spouse." However, tax law provides that investments in rental real estate are always passive with a limited exception for individuals who qualify as real estate professionals. Some limited deductions are allowed for individuals who meet an "active participation" standard. One way to qualify for active participation is to make significant management decisions. For non-real estate trade or business investments, taxpayers must meet a "material participation" standard which is much more stringent than the active participation standard in order for the income and loss from the trade or business to be considered active as opposed to passive (full discussion of these standards is beyond the scope of this guide.)

There is no indication in Pub 555 that the activity requirements for rental real estate and non-rental real estate trade or businesses are relevant for determining CP versus SP treatment of investment income from partnerships and investments in real estate. For the present, the application of this rule will be ambiguous. Taxpayers should take care to document their reasoning and collect support for whichever position they take with respect to allocation (or non-allocation) of these investment income and loss items.

Passive Activity Loss Carryforwards

Any passive loss carryforwards in existence at the time partners enter community are attributed to the partner on whose return they were generated. You **do not** split the passive activity loss carryforward between the two RDP tax returns. Once partners are in community and required to file (or choose to amend) their tax returns to reflect community property, current year passive activity losses will be reported on the return in accordance with the partnership's CP/SP status, and the passive activity loss will be calculated based on the items reported in that partner's return. Therefore, no RDP adjustment calculation is necessary for current year passive activity loss limitations or carryforwards from prior years.

CP/SP Treatment upon Disposition of Partnership or Real Estate

An open question exists regarding how the gain/loss on an active SP partnership interest (or real estate investment) is taxed upon disposition. There would seem to be three possibilities. First, since the asset is SP, the sale of the asset would generate SP income or loss. Second, since the asset has been treated as CP due to the active nature of the investment, the sale of the asset would generate CP income or loss. Finally, it is possible that the appreciation/depreciation of the asset up to the time the owner entered community would be treated as SP and any appreciation/depreciation of the asset after the owner entered community would be treated as CP. The answer to this question could further depend on facts specific to your situation. If you have this situation, you may want to consult with a tax professional or attorney prior to filing your tax returns.

Adjustments to Income

During the 2010 tax filing season, practitioners received informal guidance from the IRS that Adjustments to Income on the tax return should be treated as SP. Therefore, for the following items we suggest that you NOT split the adjustment, even if the expense was paid from CP. Since the guidance was informal, taxpayers cannot rely on the advice in case of audit.

Educator Expenses

Educators (K through 12) are allowed to deduct up to $250 of costs that they pay for classroom supplies, etc. The expenses should be reported only on the return of a partner that is an educator even if the expenses were paid with CP funds. If both partners are educators, each partner is eligible for their own $250 deduction.

Moving Expenses

Taxpayers who move a significant distance from their previous job for a new job (generally more than 50 miles – see Form 3903 for specifics) can deduct unreimbursed costs associated with the move. Since the requirements are based on moving between jobs it is possible that situations will arise where one RDP/SSMC will qualify for the moving expense deduction and the other will not. Complete Form 3903 for the qualifying RDP/SSMC and, if possible, pay moving expenses from SP funds of the qualifying RDP/SSMC to assure that the costs are eligible for the deduction.

One Half of Self-Employment Tax

This deduction is automatic and is based upon the amount of SE tax that you pay on the tax return.

SEP/IRA Deductions

IRA accounts are considered separate property for income tax purposes – even if funded with community property – so treat any allowable deductions for contributions to IRA accounts as paid by the partner in whose name the account is established. Remember, in applying the rules to determine the amount of your SEP or IRA, you are not considered married.

Self-Employed Health Insurance

If you are self-employed you may deduct health insurance payments for yourself, your spouse, and your dependents (but, your RDP/SSMC is not considered your spouse). If you deduct health insurance as an adjustment to income, remember that you may not include it as a medical expense in your itemized deductions.

Student Loan Interest & Tuition and Fees

Amounts paid for student loan interest for **you** or **your dependent** (but not your RDP/SSMC) are deductible only if your modified AGI is less than $75,000. You may be eligible for either a deduction or a credit for tuition and fees paid for you or your dependent. See Form 8917 for further details.

Medical Expenses

Medical expense deductions for RDPs/SSMCs depend on 1) whom the expenses are for and 2) how the couple will pay for the expenses - from SP or CP funds. If you did not have any major unreimbursed medical expenses during the tax year, please skip forward to read the planning point *Conserve Your Time* at the end of this section. If you or your RDP/SSMC are going to have unreimbursed major medical expenses during a tax year, please read the following section before you pay the bills.

HOW MUCH to Report - Medical Expenses

Individuals can deduct their own medical expenses as well as the medical expenses paid for their dependents and spouse. In general, you cannot automatically deduct medical expenses you pay on behalf of your RDP/SSMC because (with some limited exceptions) your RDP/SSMC *is not* your dependent or your spouse for *Federal* tax purposes. You can deduct your partner's medical expenses if your RDP/SSMC lived in your household during the year *and* you provided over one-half of your partner's support. Since CP income is considered earned one-half by each RDP/SSMC, the support requirement may be difficult to meet.

If medical expenses are paid from CP, one-half of the expenses are deemed paid by each partner. As shown in the following example, if there are significant medical expenses and/or you do not provide more than one-half of your partner's support, it may be advisable to pay those expenses from the SP funds of the RDP/SSMC receiving the medical treatment. Even when medical expenses are deductible for both partners, paying from one partner's SP may be advisable because the medical expenses will be bunched onto one tax return. In 2010, only the portion of medical expenses that exceed 7.5% of AGI may be deducted, and bunching deductions will result in more deductions in excess of the 7.5% limit.

Assume that Bartok and Hobart have a combined AGI of $100,000 that is 100% CP. Further assume that Bartok has unreimbursed medical expenses of $12,000, and Hobart has no medical expenses. Hobart does not provide more than one-half of the support for Bartok. Following are the calculations of the medical deduction for the couple.

Alternative 1 - Expenses Paid from CP

Bartok's Medical Expenses Paid from CP		
	Bartok	Hobart
AGI	$50,000	$50,000
Allowable Medical Expense	$6,000	n/a
Less: 7.5% AGI	(3,750)	n/a
Deductible Medical Expense	$2,250	n/a

If the expenses are paid from CP, Bartok will be able to deduct $2,250 (his share of the expenses paid from CP less the 7.5% AGI limitation). Although Pub 555 instructs the taxpayer to allocate one-half of the medical expenses to each RDP, Hobart will not report or deduct any of medical expenses because, although he is considered to have paid $6,000 from CP, the expenses are not a qualified medical expense for Hobart's tax return because he did not provide more than one-half of Bartok's support.

Alternative 2 - Expenses Paid from Bartok's SP

Bartok's Medical Expenses Paid from Bartok's SP		
	Bartok	Hobart
AGI	$50,000	$50,000
Allowable Medical Expense	$12,000	n/a
Less: 7.5% AGI	(3,750)	n/a
Deductible Medical Expense	$8,250	n/a

If the expenses are paid from Bartok's SP, Bartok will be able to deduct $8,250 (100% of the medical expenses paid from SP less the 7.5% AGI limitation). This results in an increase in itemized deductions of $6,000 which would save the couple approximately $1,500 in taxes.

HOW TO Report - Medical Deductions

The IRS does not currently have a matching program for tax return items like medical expenses so, unlike many of the income items, once the amount of the deduction is determined; the reporting requirements are fairly straightforward. Determine the amount of each type of medical expense (Insurance, Doctors, Prescriptions, etc.) that is properly reported by you and simply report the amounts on the appropriate lines on your tax return. You will retain the records supporting these amounts, but you do not need to show the totals and make the adjustments within the return as you do for income items.

Planning Point

Conserve Your Time - Don't Collect Data You Don't Need

In 2010, medical deductions are only allowed as an itemized deduction to the extent they exceed 7.5% of your adjusted gross income (AGI). AGI is the income amount reported on line 37 of Form 1040. Before wasting your time dredging through all of your medical paperwork, make a rough estimate of whether you will even qualify for the deduction. For instance, if your AGI is $100,000, your qualifying medical expenses must exceed $7,500 before they are deductible. Only out-of-pocket medical and insurance costs qualify. If your insurance company reimbursed you for a medical expense, it will not qualify. If your employer pays your health insurance and does not include it in your W-2 income, it will not qualify. If the medical cost is deducted elsewhere on your return, i.e., self-employed health insurance, it will not qualify.

Taxes

Itemized deductions for taxes of California RDPs will usually come from two main sources – state income taxes and real estate taxes. However, sales tax may be deducted if it is greater than the state income tax deduction so calculation of that deduction is also be covered in the following section.

State Income Taxes

Calculating the correct state income tax deduction is one of the most error prone procedures in preparing individual income tax returns. This is unfortunate since the rules for determining the deduction are fairly straightforward. In short, state income taxes are deductible in the year paid. If taxpayers can keep that rule clear, calculation of the state income tax deduction is actually easy. Problems occur because taxpayers confuse calculating the state income tax **deduction** with the amount of state income tax to be **applied as a payment** toward their current income tax. The two numbers, although related, are ususally not the same.

To illustrate calculation of the state income tax deduction, we will use an example of a typical situation. Assume that Bartok has received his W-2 and it shows $20,000 of CA withholding. In addition, assume Bartok and Hobart made the following payments to California from their CP funds:

1) Payment of $2,000 on January 15, 2010 for their 2009 4th Quarter California Estimated Taxes
2) Payment of $1,346 on April 15, 2010 for the tax due with their 2009 California Tax Return
3) Payment of $3,000 on April 15, 2010 for their 2010 1st Quarter California Estimated Taxes
4) Payment of $4,500 on January 15, 2010 for their 2010 2nd Quarter California Estimated Taxes
5) Payment of $1,000 on January 15, 2011 for their 2010 4th Quarter California Estimated Taxes

The calculation of their 2010 CA tax deduction and their 2010 CA tax payments are shown in the following figure:

| 2010 CA State Tax Deductions/Payments | Deducted on 2010 US TR | | Total | Applied to |
	Bartok	Hobart	Payments	2010 CA TR
CA 2010 Withholding	$10,000	$10,000	$20,000	$20,000
CA Estimated Payments				
2009 4th Qtr paid Jan 15, 2010	1,000	1,000	2,000	
2009 CA Tax Due April 15, 2010	673	673	1,346	
2010 1st Qtr paid April 15, 2010	1,500	1,500	3,000	3,000
2010 2nd Qtr paid June 15, 2010	2,250	2,250	4,500	4,500
2010 3rd Qtr paid Sept 15, 2010	-	-	-	-
2010 4th Qtr paid Jan 15, 2011	-	-	1,000	1,000
Total	$15,423	$15,423	$31,846	$28,500

The amount **to be deducted** for CA taxes on Bartok and Hobart's US tax returns is shown in the columns headed by their names. Since Bartok and Hobart are RDPs in California and did not complete a PPA, they will equally split the CA withholding reported on Bartok's W-2. In addition, since all of the California estimated payments were made from CP funds, the deduction for these payments will be split between the two partners. Note that the 4th quarter payment of $2,000 for the tax year 2009 was not paid until January 2010 so that payment will be deducted in 2010 even though it is actually applied as a payment toward the 2009 CA tax return. Similarly, the $1,000 4th quarter payment for 2010 was actually paid in January. Although the Bartok and Hobart will receive credit for the payment toward the taxes they owe on their 2010 California tax return, they will not deduct their share of the payment on their 2010 US tax return. Instead, they will each be able to deduct $500 on their 2011 US income tax return. The far right column shows the amount that is *applied as a payment* toward 2010 CA taxes on their joint CA return.

Sales Taxes

Taxpayers are allowed to deduct the greater of their state income tax or their state sales tax. Since California taxpayers pay a relatively high rate of state income tax, most RDPs will take the state income tax deduction rather than the sales tax deduction. Taxpayers may use either of two different methods to determine the amount of sales tax that is deductible on their tax returns - the actual method or the tax table method.

Actual Method

To deduct sales tax under the actual method, you must collect documentation for all of the sales taxes paid by you and your RDP/SSMC during the year and then determine the source from which the taxes are paid - CP or SP. Your sales tax deduction will be the sum of sales taxes paid with your SP funds plus one-half of the sales taxes paid from CP funds.

Table Method

The sales tax deduction can also be calculated by looking up the taxpayer's reported AGI in an IRS-prepared table. Since the table method depends on the taxpayer's AGI, it does not pose any implementation difficulties for RDPs/SSMCs. Most electronic tax preparation programs calculate the sales tax based on the table method and then use the greater of the table method, the actual method (if you provide the amount) or state income tax (as calculated above). If there are major purchases, such as a car, you are allowed to increase the sales tax deduction arrived at through the table method by the sales tax paid on the major purchase (1/2 if paid from CP funds). You may use the sales tax tables printed by the IRS, or you may also use the online sales tax calculator located at www.irs.gov.

Planning Point

Use the Tax Tables for Sales Tax Deduction

I suggest you use the tax tables for a several reasons. First, the amount of time necessary to track and keep the receipts to support your sales tax deduction is onerous. Second, you do not lose the sales tax deduction on large purchases - like automobiles - because the table method allows you to use the base rate for normal household expenditures PLUS the actual sales tax for large purchases. Finally, since the table amounts are based on your reported AGI, using the tables eliminates any ambiguity over whether the taxes were paid from SP or CP funds and avoids the additional calculations related to tracing the source of funds used to pay sales tax on everyday purchases.

Real Estate Taxes

In general, real estate taxes are deductible only by the owner of the property. However, the property does not have to be owned in the same ratio as the deductions are taken. Rulings have held that as long as a taxpayer has an interest in real property, payment of real estate taxes - even a non pro-rata portion of those taxes - will be deductible. The beneficial owners of residential property may also deduct real estate taxes paid on a residence. Beneficial owners are defined as those who do not have legal title to a property but do have both the burden and benefit of the property. That is, they pay the taxes - the burden - and therefore they are able to live in the property - the benefit.

The rule of beneficial ownership is important for RDPs/SSMCs because, in some cases, RDPs/

SSMCs may live in a home that is the separate property of the other partner. If real estate taxes are paid from CP, then RDPs/SSMCs are treated as each paying one-half of the taxes. Without the rule of beneficial ownership, the non-owner RDP/SSMC would not be allowed the deduction for one-half of the real estate taxes.

For instance, assume Jezebel and Rita live in a home that was purchased by Jezebel prior to becoming Rita's RDP. Since the home was purchased with SP funds prior to registration, the home is Jezebel's SP. However, if the annual real estate taxes of $4,000 are paid from Jezebel and Rita's CP funds, the taxes are assumed paid one-half by Jezebel and one-half by Rita. Without the rule of beneficial ownership, Jezebel would be allowed to deduct $2,000 in real estate taxes, and Rita would be allowed to deduct $0. But, since the rule does exist, each partner is able to deduct $2,000 in real estate taxes.

Mortgage Interest Expense

Home Mortgage Interest

One of the largest itemized deductions for taxpayers is the home mortgage interest deduction. The total amount of mortgage interest paid on a residence will usually be reported to the taxpayer on Form 1098 but depending on the circumstances, the mortgage interest may or may not be allocated between the two RDPs/SSMCs. The rules that will generally apply for determining your home mortgage deduction are essentially the same as the rules that we have previously discussed with respect to the deduction of real estate taxes.

In general, mortgage interest is deductible only by the owner of the property. However, the property does not have to be owned in the same ratio as the deductions are taken. Court cases have held that as long as a taxpayer has an interest in real property, payment of the mortgage interest on the property will be deductible. In addition, there is precedence for deducting mortgage interest by beneficial owners of the property. Beneficial owners do not have legal title to the property but they have both the burden and benefit from the property. That is, they pay the mortgage - the burden - and therefore they are able to live in the property - the benefit.

The rule of beneficial ownership is important because in some cases one partner may live in a home that is the separate property acquired by the other partner prior to registration. If mortgage interest is paid from CP, then each partner is treated as paying one-half of the interest. Without the rule of beneficial ownership, the non-owner RDP/SSMC would not be allowed the deduction for one-half of the mortgage interest.

To determine the amount of mortgage interest deduction reported on each RDPs/SSMCs tax return, you will need to determine what funds (or combination of funds) were used to pay the mortgage:

> RDP/SSMC 1's Separate Property
>
> RDP/SSMC 2's Separate Property
>
> Community Property

Let's use the following example to illustrate the possible outcomes. Assume that Jezebel and Rita own their home equally and that total interest paid during the year was $44,000. The interest was paid $20,000 by Jezebel from SP, $10,000 by Jezebel from CP, $8,000 by Rita from SP and $6,000 by Rita from CP.

Allocating Mortgage Interest Deductions

Mortgage Interest Paid	Paid From CP or SP?	Total Paid	Deducted By	
			Jezebel	Rita
Jezebel Paid	SP	$20,000	$20,000	$0
Jezebel Paid	CP	10,000	5,000	5,000
Rita Paid	SP	8,000	0	8,000
Rita Paid	CP	6,000	3,000	3,000
Total		$44,000	$28,000	$16,000

For those of you who would like to read in more detail about this particular issue, Patricia Cain's same sex tax blog (see url below) discusses some of the relevant rulings and court cases in more detail.

http://law.scu.edu/blog/samesextax/ shared-home-ownership-who-gets-to-take-interest-and-property-tax-deductions.cfm

---

Planning Point

The $1,000,000 Mortgage Limitation

In general, the home mortgage interest deduction is limited to the interest on the first $1,000,000 of home mortgage debt. An open question is whether the $1,000,000 limitation is per (unmarried) person or per property. If the limitation is based on the property, the RDPs would be limited to deductible mortgage interest on $1,000,000 mortgage debt. If the limitation is per person, then RDPs could deduct interest on as much as $2,000,000 in mortgage debt – each RDP would need to have a mortgage of $1,000,000 on the property. According to CCA 200911007 the $1,000,000 limitation applies to each property and not to each of the separate owners. However, you may wish to discuss this issue with a CPA or attorney prior to filing your tax returns.

Charitable Contributions

Cash Contributions

Cash charitable contributions do not pose a significant reporting problem for RDP/SSMC couples. If the contribution is made from CP funds, the contribution will be split between the two partners. If the contribution is made from SP funds, only the partner that funded the contribution reports the contribution. As with all other taxpayers, it is advisable to write checks for cash contributions so you have documentation in case of audit.

Cash Contributions Greater than $250

For cash contributions greater than $250 to any one charitable organization you must obtain written acknowledgement from the charity. Most charities have now established policies to provide the proper documentation and taxpayers do not usually have to make a special request to receive a letter from the charity documenting their contribution. As with cash contributions under $250, if the contribution is made from CP funds, the contribution will be split between the two partners. If the contribution is made from SP funds, only the partner that funded the contribution reports the contribution.

HOW TO Report Cash Contributions

Although you are required to maintain records of your charitable contributions, the instructions to Schedule A do not require you to list all of your cash charitable contributions nor do you need to attach any of the acknowledgements received from the charities. Most taxpayers prefer to include a list of all of the contributions but it is not required. In the case of a couple that makes both CP and SP contributions, it is easy to create an electronic spreadsheet to include with each partner's return as follows:

Cash Charitable Deductions

Charity	Paid From CP or SP?	Total Paid	Deducted By Jezebel	Deducted By Rita
United Way	CP	$1,500	$750	$750
Girl Scouts	SP - Rita	200	0	200
Campground Girls	SP - Jez	300	300	0
American Cancer Society	CP	500	250	250
Total		$2,500	$1,300	$1,200

Noncash Charitable Contributions

Noncash charitable contributions are reported separate from cash contributions but they are split in the same manner as cash contributions. If the contribution is made from CP funds, the contribution will be split between the partners. If the contribution is made from SP funds, only the partner that funded the contribution reports the contribution. The only difference between cash and noncash contributions is that there are additional documentation requirements for noncash contributions depending on the amount of the contribution.

One issue that might relate to RDPs/SSMCs is how the limitations are applied. For instance, assume that Bartok and Hobart decide to contribute playground equipment with a FMV of $450 to a charity. The equipment was originally purchased with CP funds so, the contribution is from CP. If Bartok and Hobart were married for purposes of the US Tax law, they would be making a noncash charitable deduction greater than $250 and therefore would need to meet the rules for contributions greater than $250. However, since the Federal law does not recognize Bartok and Hobart as a married couple, they are each assumed to make a contribution of $225 since they split the contribution. To support their contribution, it would probably be best if the charity could issue two letters – one to each partner acknowledging one-half of the contribution. Alternatively, the couple should make sure the charity lists both partners on the acknowledgement if only one letter is sent by the charity.

To report the contributions, complete a worksheet similar to the worksheet shown under cash contributions. Following are the basic requirements for noncash charitable contributions of varying amounts. If you make large noncash charitable contributions, please see PUB 526 to make sure you meet all of the reporting requirements.

Less than $250

Receipt is not required (but is good practice).

$250 to $500

Written acknowledgement from Charity is required.

$501 to $5,000

Written acknowledgement from Charity is required PLUS records must show how property was acquired, the date acquired, and the adjusted basis of the property. **Must file Form 8283.**

Greater than $5,000

Written acknowledgement from Charity is required PLUS records must show how property was acquired, the date acquired, and the adjusted basis of the property. Most contributions over $5,000 require an appraisal. **Must file Form 8283.**

Filing Your Tax Returns with the IRS

Special Forms to Include with RDP Returns

Once you have completed your tax returns, you will need to paper file them with the IRS. Because of your filing status as RDPs/SSMCs, you will need to attach additional information to the paper copy of the return. We suggest that you file your return assembled in the following order:

1. RDP/SSMC Cover Sheet*
2. Federal Withholding Worksheet*
3. Copies of W-2s for Both Partners
4. Tax Return
5. Pub 555 Worksheet*
6. Other attachments/elections

See Appendix D for examples of forms marked with *. Also, editable versions of these forms will be available for you to download from my website:

www.flanerycpa.com

The IRS has specifically requested that you

1. do not file the returns together in one envelope and
2. do not attach a copy of your partner's tax return to your tax return.

File each return in its own, separate envelope even if both are going to the same address.

Where to File

The filing addresses for paper returns filed by California State Residents are:

If you *are including* a check or money order:

Internal Revenue Service

P.O. Box 1214

San Francisco, CA 94120-7704

If you *are not including* a check or money order:

Department of the Treasury

Internal Revenue Service

Fresno, CA 93888-0002

Preparation of California RDP/SSMC Joint Tax Return

California RDPs and SSMCs must prepare 3 distinct tax returns,

1) Partner 1's US Individual Income tax return declaring a filing status of Single or HOH
2) Partner 2's US Individual Income tax return declaring a filing status of Single or HOH
3) California Individual Income tax return declaring Married/RDP filing joint[2]

Approach to Return Preparation

In preparing the tax returns, it is sometimes easier to prepare the joint California tax return FIRST and then prepare the two individual Federal Tax returns. This is particularly true if you are using an electronic tax preparation program to prepare the returns. California allows RDPs/SSMCs to prepare the California tax return two different ways 1) prepare a *pro forma* federal tax return AS IF you were allowed to prepare and file a married filing joint tax return for federal purposes or 2) prepare a California RDP *adjustments worksheet* that lists the amounts reported on each partner's federal return and then shows adjustments to these amounts to arrive at an adjusted federal total that is then used in preparation of the California tax return. When prepared correctly, both methods will arrive at the same amount of California taxable income. We will present the *pro forma* method in this Guide. In addition, we assume you will use some type of electronic tax preparation program. Only the simplest returns should be prepared by hand. The reason we choose this method is that many of the adjustments that you must make in order to file a correct California tax return will automatically be made if you prepare a pro forma US tax return using an electronic tax program.

Pro forma Method of California Tax Return Preparation

As with the federal tax return, we will not discuss every adjustment that may need to be made on the California return but we will cover the most common adjustments. Many of the adjustments made for the Federal tax return were simply determining how to split the Federal amounts between the two partners. If an item was simply split between the two taxpayers, then the California return for that item is straightforward; the two amounts are added together and reported as one sum. However, filing a joint return will result in a different AGI being reported and any income or deduction item that is based on AGI will need to be recalculated using the pro forma AGI. The goal of pro forma Federal Return is to calculate Federal taxable income "AS IF" the RDPs/SSMCs were recognized as married for Federal tax purposes. The California return then uses the pro forma Federal return as the starting point for calculating California taxable income.

---

[2] RDPs and SSMCs may also file separately in California however this option is usually not advantageous to the couple. If you choose this option or would like to verify whether it will result in tax savings simply prepare a California return using the MFS filing status for each partner using the same numbers as the separate US Income tax returns.

Wages Adjustment for Partner's Health Benefits

California law employer benefit programs allow their employees to obtain health benefits for their RDP or SSMC partners. Some employers include this benefit in the federal wages of the employee. If the employer *has* included this benefit as taxable wages, the income reported for California should be reduced accordingly. There are several ways to make this adjustment. However, one easy way to do this for your pro forma federal return is to create a second W-2 input sheet in your electronic tax return program and enter a negative in wages equal to the amount of the partner health benefit income. Another way to achieve the same result is to simply adjust the amount of W-2 income reported to equal the total W-2 income less the partner health benefit income.

Capital Gains and Losses

Since RDPs and SSMCs file separate US income tax returns, they are each allowed a maximum net capital loss of $3,000. However, for purposes of the California pro forma federal return, the partners will be limited to a combined $3,000 of capital loss. The couple will report all of their gains and losses on the pro forma federal return and calculate the net gain or loss accordingly. If there is a net loss, it is limited to $3,000 and the remainder of the loss is carried forward. This difference between federal and California reporting can result in a difference between the gain/loss recognized on the federal and California tax returns as well as the amount of capital loss carryforward reported on the two returns. For instance, assume that Rita and Jezebel need to report the following gains and losses on their Federal and California tax returns:

Summary of Jezebel & Rita's Net Gains and Losses

Description	ST or LT	CP or SP	Gain (Loss)
Stock Sale A	LT	CP	$1,000
Stock Sale B	LT	Jez - SP	(2,000)
Stock Sale C	LT	Jez - SP	(2,500)
Stock Sale D	LT	Rita - SP	750
Total			($2,750)

The net loss for all transactions during the year is a net loss of $2,750 but, as previously discussed, because the gains and losses must be split between the two federal tax returns based on their ownership classification (CP or SP) and therefore the amount that will be reported on the two returns in the current year may not sum to a loss of $2,750. Assuming that there are no capital loss carryforwards to consider from prior years, Jezebel would report the following on her Federal tax return.

How Much to Report - Jezebel's Federal Tax Return

Description	ST or LT	CP or SP	Gain (Loss)
Stock Sale A	LT	CP	$500
Stock Sale B	LT	Jez - SP	(2,000)
Stock Sale C	LT	Jez - SP	(2,500)
Stock Sale D	LT	Rita - SP	n/a
Total			($4,000)

Report as:

Capital Loss Deduction on 2010 TR	($3,000)
Capital Loss Carryforward to 2011 TR	($1,000)

Jezebel would actually report a net loss for the year but, because net long term capital losses are limited to $3,000 in a single year, Jezebel would report a $3,000 on her 2010 Federal tax return and have a $1,000 long term capital loss carryforward that would be used in preparing her 2011 federal tax return.

Rita would report one-half of the CP stock sale plus her SP stock sale on her 2010 Federal tax return.

How Much to Report - Rita's Federal Tax Return

Description	ST or LT	CP or SP	Gain (Loss)
Stock Sale A	LT	CP	$500
Stock Sale B	LT	Jez - SP	n/a
Stock Sale C	LT	Jez - SP	n/a
Stock Sale D	LT	Rita - SP	750
Total			$1,250

So, for Federal purposes Jezebel and Rita would report a net loss of only $1,750 between their two returns and Jezebel would have a capital loss carryforward of $1,000 to her 2011 tax return. However, on their California tax return, Jezebel and Rita would report the following:

How Much to Report - Joint Pro-Forma Federal/California

Description	ST or LT	CP or SP	Gain (Loss)
Stock Sale A	LT	CP	$1,000
Stock Sale B	LT	Jez - SP	(2,000)
Stock Sale C	LT	Jez - SP	(2,500)
Stock Sale D	LT	Rita - SP	750
Total			($2,750)

The pro forma Federal/CA returns would not report a capital loss carryforward to 2011 because the capital loss calculated on the joint return would not exceed $3,000. If you are using an electronic tax preparation program and follow our instructions to prepare the pro forma Federal/CA tax return using the software, the program will calculate the correct gain/loss for the California return.

Transactions Between RDPs

Since RDPs and SSMCs are recognized as married under California law, certain transactions between partners that are recognized for Federal tax purposes are not recognized for California tax purposes. This difference in taxation will also result in a difference in basis for Federal and California purposes (see discussion of gift and estate tax in introductory material for a brief description of the Federal gift tax rules).

For example, since RDPs/SSMCs are not related parties for Federal tax purposes, sales of property between the partners may create a taxable gain or loss. Assume Bartok inherited some land several years ago. Since the land was inherited, it is Bartok's SP. Bartok sold the land to an unrelated party this year and recognizes a capital gain of $40,000. Bartok also has some stock that is SP. Bartok's basis in the stock is $50,000 and it has a market value of $15,000. If Bartok sells the stock he could recognize a loss of $35,000 and use the loss to partially offset the $40,000 capital gain. But, Bartok believes the stock's value is going to increase and he really doesn't want to dispose of it so he decides to sell the stock to Hobart and recognize the loss. This way, Bartok believes he will get to recognize the large capital loss and use it to offset the capital gain but Hobart, his RDP, will still own the stock.

Since Hobart and Bartok's relationship is not recognized for federal tax purposes, Bartok will recognize the $35,000 loss and Hobart will have stock with basis equal to $15,000, the amount he paid for it from his SP funds. However, since Bartok and Hobart's relationship IS recognized for California tax purposes, Bartok will not be able to recognize the loss on the stock sale (due to the related party transaction rules) so he will have a gain of $40,000 on the Land and no loss to offset the gain on his California return. In addition, the basis of the stock will not be $15,000 but $50,000 for California tax purposes. Bartok and Hobart will have to track this difference between the Federal and California basis in the stock until the stock is actually sold to a non-related 3rd party.

Basis differences between Federal and California will also occur when gifts are made between the partners since the transactions between RDPs/SSMCs will be considered gifts for Federal tax purposes but not California tax purposes.

Sale of Residence

If RDPs/SSMCs sell their jointly owned principal residence they are allowed to exclude up to $250,000 of gain on each of their Federal tax returns – the exact amount excluded by each RDP/SSMC will depend on each partner's share of ownership in the home and each partner's basis in the home. If one RDP/SSMC owns the residence as SP, then only that partner can exclude gain on their Federal tax return. However, if a California Married/RDP Filing Joint return is filed, the couple is able to exclude up to $500,000 of gain on the pro forma Federal/CA tax return.

Social Security Benefits

The amount of social security benefits that are included in taxable income will depend on the total amount of social security and other income that is reported. Since the pro forma return will report income and benefits from both partners, the portion of social security benefit that is taxable will probably increase in the joint return (assuming combining the separate returns results in higher total income). If you prepare a pro forma joint Federal return, the electronic tax software will calculate the correct taxable benefit for California joint return.

Expense Depreciation Property Limitations

Small businesses may elect to deduct the cost of some business property in accordance with Sec 179 rather than expense it. If both RDPs/SSMCs elect to deduct costs under Sec 179 on their separately filed Federal returns, they may be limited on the deduction on their joint California tax return. The limit applies per tax return, not per taxpayer. Therefore, for purposes of preparing the Federal Pro Forma tax return, you may need to recalculate the Sec 179 deduction. The deduction will be limited only if the sum of the Sec 179 deduction taken on both returns exceeds the single return limit. With recent increases in the Sec 179 limit, it is unlikely that most individual taxpayers will be limited. In 2010, the Sec 179 limit was $500,000 (however, this amount is reduced if qualifying purchases exceed $2,000,000.)

Rental Real Estate Passive Losses

For Federal tax purposes, taxpayers are allowed to deduct up to $25,000 of passive activity losses if their modified AGI is less than $100,000. The deduction is then phased out for modified AGI greater than $100,000. Any passive activity losses limited due to this rule can be carried forward and used against future passive income or deducted when the activity is sold. Since RDPs/SSMCs file a joint tax return for California, it is more likely that their combined AGI will be greater than $100,000 therefore requiring the passive losses to be limited on the California joint return. In addition, if there is a difference between the amount of passive loss allowed on the separate Federal and joint California tax returns, the passive activity loss carryforwards will also be different for the separate Federal and California tax returns. If you prepare a pro forma Federal return using an electronic tax preparation program, this amount will be calculated on Form 8582.

Individual Retirement Accounts

Contributions made to traditional IRAs by one or both of the partners on their individual Federal returns must be re-evaluated for purposes of the pro forma Federal/CA tax return. Since the modified AGI on the pro forma Federal return will usually be greater than the AGI on the separately filed Federal returns, the IRA deductions may be limited due to the higher AGI. If the RDP contributing to a traditional IRA was covered by an employee retirement plan, the IRA deduction will begin to be phased out at a modified AGI of $89,000 on the Married/RDP Filing Joint return. If the RDP contribution to a traditional IRA *is not* covered by an employee retirement plan but the employee's partner *was* covered by an employee retirement plan, the IRA deduction will begin to be phased out at a modified AGI of $167,000 on the Married/RDP Filing Joint return.

Education Loan Interest

There are two limitations associated with interest on education loans that may be affected by combining the two partner's individual Federal tax returns to a pro forma federal/CA tax return. First, education interest is limited to $2,500 on the 2010 tax return so, if both partners reported educational loan interest, they may find that the combined interest is greater than $2,500 limit and a portion of the interest will be disallowed. Second, the education interest deduction is phased out on joint returns for modified AGIs between $120,000 and $150,000. To determine the amount of this deduction on your joint California return you must recalculate it subject to these limits on your pro forma Federal return.

Dependent Care Assistance

Tax benefits related to dependent care expenses may be limited on the joint CA return when compared to the couples' separately filed Federal returns. In general, up to $5,000 of dependent care expenses may be deducted (or excluded from income if reimbursed by employer). If each RDP/SSMC was able to report dependent care assistance costs, then the amounts paid for dependent care must be reported on one return and deducted in accordance with the combined reporting on the pro forma Federal/CA return. If the combined amount from the separate returns filed by the RDPs/SSMCs exceeds $5,000 there will be an adjustment for the federal pro forma/CA tax return.

Medical and Dental Expenses

Medical and dental expenses paid by one partner for the other partner or their dependents are deductible for purposes of preparing the pro forma Federal/CA tax return. However, the AGI limitation will be based on the new combined AGI reported on the pro forma Federal/CA return.

Qualified Residence Acquisition Loan & Equity Loan Interest

On the pro forma Federal/CA tax returns interest on acquisition indebtedness is limited to the interest on acquisition debt of $1,000,000. If the taxpayers took a position that allowed the RDPs/SSMCs to deduct interest on their separately filed Federal tax returns that would exceed this limitation on the joint pro forma tax returns, the interest deduction must be adjusted.

Similarly, RDPs/SSMCs are allowed to deduct interest only on the first $100,000 of home equity indebtedness on their pro forma Federal/CA tax return.

Job and Miscellaneous Deductions subject to 2%

Since AGI on the pro forma Federal/CA return will be different than on the separately filed Federal returns, the job and miscellaneous deductions subject to 2% must be combined and then only the portion that exceeds 2% of the pro forma AGI may be deducted.

Filing Your Tax Returns with California FTB

Filing Copy of California Return and Attachments

Once you have completed your pro forma federal tax returns and the California Joint tax return based on the pro forma Federal return, you will need to paper file the California return with the FTB. Because of your filing status as RDPs/SSMCs, you will need to attach additional information to the paper copy of the return. We suggest that you file your return assembled in the following order:

1. California Married/RDP Joint Tax Return
2. Copies of W-2s for Both Partners
3. Pro forma Married Filing Joint US Tax Return for couple
4. US Tax Return – RDP/SSMC #1 as originally filed
5. US Tax Return – RDP/SSMC #2 as originally filed

Filing California Joint Tax Return

If you *are including* a check or money order:

Franchise Tax Board

P.O. Box 942867

Sacramento, CA 94267-0001

If you *are not including* a check or money order:

Franchise Tax Board

P.O.Box 942840

Sacramento, CA 94240-0002

Responding to IRS Notices

Let me start by making two points.

First, I understand that few things are more stressful for a taxpayer than receiving mail - any kind of mail - from the IRS. However, the important thing to know is that MOST IRS correspondence does not contain bad news.

Second, even though you are required to file as an RDP, this filing status will in all probability result in your receiving notices from the IRS because the electronic matching system was not designed to deal with community property income and deductions being split across two tax returns.

What to Do if You Receive IRS Correspondence

If you receive correspondence from the IRS, the best advice I can give you is

1. open and read the letter as soon as you get it, and then

2. respond to the letter within the period given to you by the IRS.

If you follow both of these recommendations, most of these notices will be resolved with little effort. The majority of problems I have had dealing with the IRS on behalf of clients is not from the notices but from the fact that clients did not respond to the notices in a timely manner. The more response deadlines you miss, the harder, and more expensive, it will be to solve the problem.

Types of IRS Correspondence

Almost all IRS correspondence is generated by a computer and will fall into one of the following 4 categories:

1. General Correspondence

   This is mail that is sent to everybody. These letters usually tell you something like, "Congress just passed a new tax law, and we won't have the forms ready until March 12th." These letters have nothing to do with you specifically, and require no response.

2. Helpful Correspondence

   This correspondence is sent directly to you based on some criteria the computer identified in your tax return. The IRS may send you forms or publications that they think you might need. For instance, if you had to make a payment with your tax return on April 15th, the computer might decide that you should consider making quarterly estimated tax payments. To help you, the computer will send you the estimated tax vouchers and the instructions for making estimated tax payments. You haven't done anything wrong; they are just being proactive and trying to make sure you don't have an underpayment penalty in the current year. Read the information to see if it applies to your situation and then act accordingly.

3. Matching Notices

> These notices require a response. They are usually computer generated and will simply contain a table of items listing a) what they think was included on your tax return and b) what they think should have been included on the tax return. Your response will consist of a copy of the relevant forms from your filed tax return and an explanation of where on your return you reported the items that they are confused about. In many cases, the problem is simply that the "missing" items are $1 different due to rounding or the Payor name reported to the IRS was different than the name listed on the tax return (see a sample response letter below).

4. Audit & Other Notifications

> These notices require a response. Just because you are being audited does not mean the IRS has targeted you. The computer randomly generates most audit notices. If you have honestly completed your tax return, have the supporting records for your income and deductions, and respond within the time limits you are given, you should not anticipate insurmountable problems.

Responding to IRS Matching Notices

When responding to an IRS notice, the goal is to make it as easy as possible for the IRS employee to understand your response. ALWAYS attach a copy of the IRS notice to your response. ALWAYS include a copy of any relevant schedules that you refer to from your tax return. ALWAYS include supporting detail for your numbers if you have it (Forms 1099, 1098, etc.). For the sample on the following page, assume the IRS sent you a notice stating the following:

"We show $800 of interest from Wells Fargo and $10,000 of mortgage interest expense paid to UBS. We have adjusted your tax return to reflect these amounts."

Further assume that you actually reported $400 of interest on your tax return from Wells Fargo and $5,000 of mortgage interest expense paid to UBS because your RDP reported the other half of these amounts. Following is a sample letter that could be sent to the IRS to explain the situation and request that the tax return be accepted as originally filed.

Sample Response Letter to IRS Notice

Department of the Treasury

Internal Revenue Service

(Response Address given on the notice)

July 10, 2011

RE: Taxpayer Name & SSN

Dear Sir or Madam:

I am writing in response to your notice dated July 1, 2011 (copy attached), in which you propose adjustments to my tax return. In the notice you state that I failed to report $800 in interest income from Wells Fargo and $10,000 in mortgage interest expense from UBS.

In fact, I did properly report the interest income and mortgage interest expense on my tax return. I am a registered domestic partner domiciled in California. CCA 201021050 requires my partner and me to split our community property income and deductions paid from community property. Since my partner and I were registered prior to 2010, our income was subject to the community property rules for the entire year.

Interest income from Wells Fargo was reported as follows:

Taxpayer 1 – SSN 1	$ 400
Taxpayer 2 – SSN 2	400
Total Reported	$ 800

Copies of Schedule B for Taxpayer 1 and Taxpayer 2 as originally filed are included for your review.

Mortgage interest expense from UBS was reported as follows:

Taxpayer 1 – SSN 1	$ 5,000
Taxpayer 2 – SSN 2	5,000
Total Reported	$10,000

Copies of Schedule A for Taxpayer 1 and Taxpayer 2 as originally filed are included for your review.

Therefore, as required by CCA 201021050, all of the interest income and mortgage expense was reported. Based on the above information, I respectfully request that you accept the return as originally filed. Thank you in advance for your attention to this matter. Please do not hesitate to contact the undersigned if you should have any questions or concerns.

Sincerely,

J. Q. Citizen, Taxpayer

Abbreviations

AGI – Adjusted Gross Income

CA - California

CCA – Chief Council's Advice

CD – Certificate of Deposit

CP – Community Property

DOMA - Defense of Marriage Act

ESA – Education Savings Account

FTB – Franchise Tax Board

HOH - Head of Household Filing Status

IRA – Individual Retirement Account

IRS – Internal Revenue Service

LTCG – Long Term Capital Gain

LTCL – Long Term Capital Loss

MFJ - Married Filing Joint

MFS - Married Filing Separate

PPA – Pre (or Post) -Partnership Agreement

RDP - Washington, Nevada, California Registered Domestic Partners (in general)

S - Single

SE – Self-Employment/Self-Employed

SEP – Simplified Employee Pension

SP – Separate Property

SSMC – Same-Sex Married Couple

SSN – Social Security Number

STCG – Short Term Capital Gain

STCL – Short Term Capital Loss

YTD – Year-to-Date

About the Author

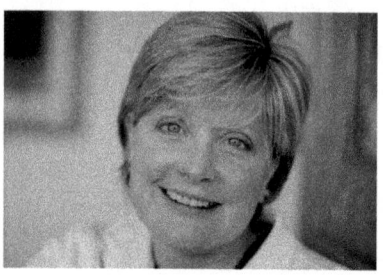

Marci Flanery is a CPA specializing in the taxation of individuals and their related small business entities. Marci's tax practice has locations in San Francisco and the Westlake/Denny neighborhood of Seattle.

Marci became a CPA in 1984 and worked for 8 years in the Kansas City and Seattle Offices of Arthur Andersen & Co. After leaving AA & Co., she taught for 8 years in the accounting program at the University of Kansas. Marci then moved to Nashville, TN to earn her PhD in Cognitive Psychology from Vanderbilt University. After graduate school, Marci completed post-doctoral work in the Neuroimaging of Memory and Cognition at Johns Hopkins University in Baltimore, MD before moving to California and returning to the practice of public accounting.

Before starting her own tax practice, Marci worked in the San Francisco office of one of the city's premier tax firms specializing in the taxation of RDPs. During this time, Marci was responsible for tax planning and tax return preparation for hundreds of California RDP and Same-Sex Married couples.

Marci is a licensed CPA in Missouri, California, and Washington with decades of experience as a tax consultant specializing in individual and small business tax preparation and planning. She is accepting a limited number of new clients to her Seattle practice.

For more information about Marci's tax practice and updates to the Guide:

marci@flanerycpa.com

www.flanerycpa.com

Updates and Corrections

A list of updates, corrections, and other errata related to the Guide will be maintained on my website: www.flanerycpa.com.

A new edition of the Guide will be released in January of each year. The new edition will incorporate corrections to previous editions in addition to addressing any changes in the tax law regarding RDP/SSMC couples since publication of the prior year's Guide.

Appendix A - CCA 201021050

Office of Chief Counsel
Internal Revenue Service
memorandum

Number: **201021050**
Release Date: 5/28/2010

PRESP-111796-10

UILC: 61.00-00, 61.31-00

date: May 05, 2010

to: Cheryl Sherwood
       Director, Campus Compliance Services, SB:S:CCS:CRC

       Brady Bennett
       Director, Compliance SE:W:C

from: Michael J. Montemurro
       Branch Chief
       Office of Associate Chief Counsel
       (Income Tax & Accounting)

subject: California Registered Domestic Partners

On February 24, 2006, the Office of Associate Chief Counsel (Income Tax & Accounting) issued Chief Counsel Advice (CCA) 200608038 concluding that an individual who is a registered domestic partner in California must report all of his or her income earned from the performance of personal services. In light of a change to California law, effective in 2007, you asked us whether California registered domestic partners should each report half of the community income on their federal returns. You also asked whether individuals who filed returns in accordance with CCA 200608038 must amend those returns.

FACTS

In 2005, California law significantly expanded the rights and obligations of persons entering into a California domestic partnership for state property law purposes, but not for state income tax purposes. Specifically, the California Domestic Partner Rights and Responsibilities Act of 2003 (the California Act), effective on January 1, 2005, provided that "Registered domestic partners shall have the same rights, protections, and benefits, and shall be subject to the same responsibilities, obligations, and duties under law . . . as are granted to and imposed upon spouses." However, the California Act provided that "earned income may not be treated as community property for state income tax purposes."

PRESP-111796-10

On September 29, 2006, California enacted Senate Bill 1827. Senate Bill 1827 repealed the language of the California Act providing that earned income was not to be

treated as community property for state income tax purposes. Thus, effective January 1, 2007, the earned income of a registered domestic partner must be treated as community property for state income tax purposes (unless the RDPs execute an agreement opting out of community property treatment). As a result of the legislation, California, as of January 1, 2007, treats the earned income of registered domestic partners as community property for both property law purposes and state income tax purposes.

LAW AND ANALYSIS

Section 61(a)(1) of the Internal Revenue Code provides that gross income means all income from whatever source derived including compensation for services such as fees, commissions, fringe benefits, and similar items.

Federal tax law generally respects state property law characterizations and definitions. *U.S. v. Mitchell*, 403 U.S. 190 (1971), *Burnet v. Harmel*, 287 U.S. 103 (1932). In *Poe v. Seaborn*, 282 U.S. 101 (1930), the Supreme Court held that for federal income tax purposes a wife owned an undivided one-half interest in the income earned by her husband in Washington, a community property state, and was liable for federal income tax on that one-half interest. Accordingly, the Court concluded that husband and wife must each report one-half of the community income on his or her separate return regardless of which spouse earned the income. *United States v. Malcolm*, 282 U.S. 792 (1931), applied the rule of *Poe v. Seaborn* to California's community property law.

California community property law developed in the context of marriage and originally applied only to the property rights and obligations of spouses. The law operated to give each spouse an equal interest in each community asset, regardless of which spouse is the holder of record. *d'Elia v. d'Elia*, 58 Cal. App. 4th 415 (1997).

By 2007, California had extended *full community property treatment* [1] to registered domestic partners. Applying the principle that federal law respects state law property characterizations, the federal tax treatment of community property should apply to California registered domestic partners. Consequently, for tax years beginning after December 31, 2006, a California registered domestic partner must report one-half of the community income, whether received in the form of compensation for personal services or income from property, on his or her federal income tax return.

---

[1] Prior to January 1, 2007, the earned income of a registered domestic partner was treated as community property for state property law purposes but not for state income tax purposes.

3

PRESP-111796-10

You also asked how to treat a registered domestic partner who reported all of his or her earned income in accordance with CCA 200608038. For tax years beginning before June 1, 2010, registered domestic partners may, but are not required to, amend their returns to report income in accordance with this CCA.

Please call Shareen Pflanz or Steve Toomey at (202) 622-4920 if you have any questions concerning this memorandum.

Appendix B - IRS Publication 555

Department of the Treasury
Internal Revenue Service

Publication 555
(Rev. December 2010)

Cat. No. 15103C

Community Property

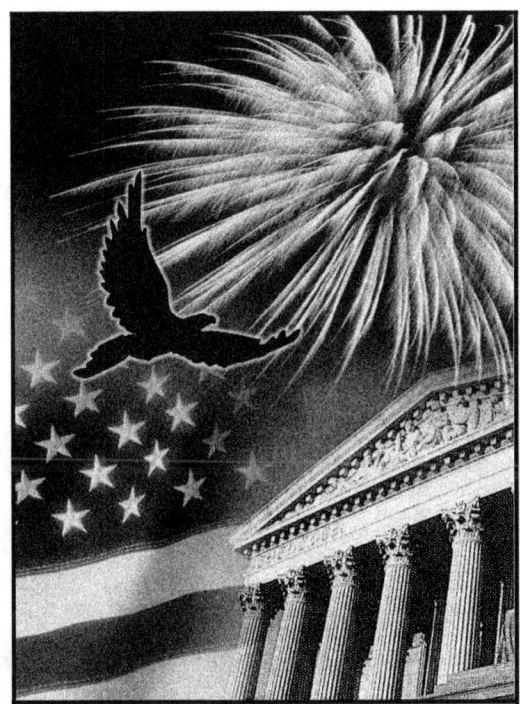

Get forms and other information faster and easier by:

Internet IRS.gov

Contents

Important Reminder

Photographs of missing children. The Internal Revenue Service is a proud partner with the National Center for Missing and Exploited Children. Photographs of missing children selected by the Center may appear in this publication on pages that would otherwise be blank. You can help bring these children home by looking at the photographs and calling 1-800-THE-LOST (1-800-843-5678) if you recognize a child.

Introduction

This publication is for married taxpayers who are domiciled in one of the following community property states:

- Arizona,
- California,
- Idaho,
- Louisiana,
- Nevada,
- New Mexico,
- Texas,
- Washington, or
- Wisconsin.

Feb 24, 2011

This publication does not address the federal tax treatment of income or property subject to the "community property" election under Alaska state laws.

Community property laws affect how you figure your income on your federal income tax return if you are married, live in a community property state or country, and file separate returns. For federal tax purposes, a marriage means only a legal union between a man and woman as husband and wife and the word "spouse" refers only to a person of the opposite sex who is a husband or a wife. If you are married, your tax usually will be less if you file married filing jointly than if you file married filing separately. However, sometimes it can be to your advantage to file separate returns. If you and your spouse file separate returns, you have to determine your community income and your separate income.

Community property laws also affect your basis in property you inherit from a married person who lived in a community property state. See *Death of spouse*, later.

Nevada, Washington, and California domestic partners. This publication is also for registered domestic partners (RDPs) who are domiciled in Nevada, Washington, or California and for individuals in California who, for state law purposes, are married to an individual of the same sex. For 2010, a RDP in Nevada, Washington, or California (or a person in California who is married to a person of the same sex) generally must follow state community property laws and report half the combined community income of the individual and his or her RDP (or California same-sex spouse).

These rules apply to RDPs in Nevada, Washington, and California in 2010 because they have full community property rights in 2010. California RDPs attained these rights as of January 1, 2007. Nevada RDPs attained them as of October 1, 2009, and Washington RDPs attained them as of June 12, 2008. For years prior to 2010, RDPs who reported income without regard to the community property laws may file amended returns to report half of the community income of the RDPs for the applicable periods, but are not required to do so. If one of the RDPs files an amended return to report half of the community income, the other RDP must report the other half.

RDPs (and individuals in California who are married to an individual of the same sex) are not married for federal tax purposes. They can use only the single filing status, or if they qualify, the head of household filing status.

Comments and suggestions. We welcome your comments about this publication and your suggestions for future editions.

You can write to us at the following address:

Internal Revenue Service
Individual Forms and Publications Branch
SE:W:CAR:MP:T:I
1111 Constitution Ave. NW, IR-6526
Washington, DC 20224

We respond to many letters by telephone. Therefore, it would be helpful if you would include your daytime phone number, including the area code, in your correspondence.

You can email us at *taxforms@irs.gov*. (The asterisk must be included in the address.) Please put "Publications Comment" on the subject line. Although we cannot respond individually to each email, we do appreciate your feedback and will consider your comments as we revise our tax products.

Ordering forms and publications. Visit *www.irs.gov/ formspubs* to download forms and publications, call 1-800-829-3676, or write to the address below and receive a response within 10 days after your request is received.

Internal Revenue Service
1201 N. Mitsubishi Motorway
Bloomington, IL 61705-6613

Tax questions. If you have a tax question, check the information available at IRS.gov or call 1-800-829-1040. We cannot answer tax questions sent to either of the addresses earlier on this page.

Useful Items

You may want to see:

Publication

❑ **504** Divorced or Separated Individuals

❑ **505** Tax Withholding and Estimated Tax

❑ **971** Innocent Spouse Relief

Form (and Instructions)

❑ **8857** Request for Innocent Spouse Relief

See *How To Get Tax Help* near the end of this publication for information about getting these publications.

Domicile

Whether you have community property and community income depends on the state where you are domiciled. If you and your spouse (or RDP/California same-sex spouse) have different domiciles, check the laws of each to see whether you have community property or community income.

You have only one domicile even if you have more than one home. Your domicile is a permanent legal home that you intend to use for an indefinite or unlimited period, and to which, when absent, you intend to return. The question of your domicile is mainly a matter of your intention as indicated by your actions. You must be able to show with facts that you intend a given place or state to be your permanent home. If you move into or out of a community property state during the year, you may or may not have community income.

Factors considered in determining domicile include:

- Where you pay state income tax,

- Where you vote,

- Location of property you own,

- Your citizenship,

- Length of residence, and

- Business and social ties to the community.

Amount of time spent. The amount of time spent in one place does not always explain the difference between home and domicile. A temporary home or residence may continue for months or years while a domicile may be established the first moment you occupy the property. Your intent is the determining factor in proving where you have your domicile.

Note. When this publication refers to where you live, it means your domicile.

Community or Separate Property and Income

If you file a federal tax return separately from your spouse, you must report half of all community income and all of your separate income. Likewise, a RDP (and an individual in California who is married to an individual of the same sex) must report half of all community income and all of his or her separate income on his or her federal tax return. Generally, the laws of the state in which you are domiciled govern whether you have community property and community income or separate property and separate income

for federal tax purposes. The following is a summary of the general rules. These rules are also shown in Table 1.

Community property. Generally, community property is property:

- That you, your spouse (or RDP/California same-sex spouse), or both acquire during your marriage (or registered domestic partnership/same-sex marriage in California) while you and your spouse (or RDP/California same-sex spouse) are domiciled in a community property state.

- That you and your spouse (or RDP/California same-sex spouse) agreed to convert from separate to community property.

- That cannot be identified as separate property.

Community income. Generally, community income is income from:

- Community property.

- Salaries, wages, and other pay received for the services performed by you, your spouse (or RDP/California same-sex spouse), or both during your marriage

Table 1. **General Rules — Property and Income: Community or Separate?**

Community property is property:	**Separate property** is:
• That you, your spouse (or RDP/California same-sex spouse), or both acquire during your marriage (or registered domestic partnership/same-sex marriage in California) while you are domiciled in a community property state. (Includes the part of property bought with community property funds if part was bought with community funds and part with separate funds.) • That you and your spouse (or RDP/California same-sex spouse) agreed to convert from separate to community property. • That cannot be identified as separate property.	• Property that you or your spouse (or RDP/California same-sex spouse) owned separately before your marriage (or registered domestic partnership/same-sex marriage in California). • Money earned while domiciled in a noncommunity property state. • Property either of you received as a gift or inherited separately during your marriage (or registered domestic partnership/same-sex marriage in California). • Property bought with separate funds, or exchanged for separate property, during your marriage (or registered domestic partnership/same-sex marriage in California). • Property that you and your spouse (or RDP/California same-sex spouse) agreed to convert from community to separate property through an agreement valid under state law. • The part of property bought with separate funds, if part was bought with community funds and part with separate funds.
Community income [1,2,3] is income from: • Community property. • Salaries, wages, or pay for services of you, your spouse (or RDP/California same-sex spouse), or both during your marriage (or registered domestic partnership/same-sex marriage in California). • Real estate that is treated as community property under the laws of the state where the property is located.	**Separate income** [1,2] is income from: • Separate property. Separate income belongs to the spouse (or RDP/California same-sex spouse) who owns the property.

[1] **Caution:** In Idaho, Louisiana, Texas, and Wisconsin, income from most separate property is community income.
[2] **Caution:** Check your state law if you are separated but do not meet the conditions discussed in *Spouses living apart all year.* In some states, the income you earn after you are separated and before a divorce decree is issued continues to be community income. In other states, it is separate income.
[3] **Caution:** Under special rules, income that can otherwise be characterized as community income may not be treated as community income for federal income tax purposes in certain situations. See *Community Property Laws Disregarded,* later.

(or registered domestic partnership/same-sex marriage in California).

- Real estate that is treated as community property under the laws of the state where the property is located.

Separate property. Generally, separate property is:

- Property that you or your spouse (or RDP/California same-sex spouse) owned separately before your marriage (or registered domestic partnership/same-sex marriage in California).

- Money earned while domiciled in a noncommunity property state.

- Property that you or your spouse (or RDP/California same-sex spouse) received separately as a gift or inheritance during your marriage (or registered domestic partnership/same-sex marriage in California).

- Property that you or your spouse (or RDP/California same-sex spouse) bought with separate funds, or acquired in exchange for separate property, during your marriage (or registered domestic partnership/same-sex marriage in California).

- Property that you and your spouse (or RDP/California same-sex spouse) converted from community property to separate property through an agreement valid under state law.

- The part of property bought with separate funds, if part was bought with community funds and part with separate funds.

Separate income. Generally, income from separate property is the separate income of the spouse (or RDP/California same-sex spouse) who owns the property.

 In Idaho, Louisiana, Texas, and Wisconsin, income from most separate property is community income.

Identifying Income, Deductions, and Credits

If you file separate returns, you and your spouse (or RDP/California same-sex spouse) must be able to identify your community and separate income, deductions, credits, and other return amounts according to the laws of your state.

Income

The following is a discussion of the general effect of community property laws on the federal income tax treatment of certain items of income.

Wages, earnings, and profits. A spouse's (or RDP's/California same-sex spouse's) wages, earnings, and net profits from a sole proprietorship are community income and must be evenly split.

Dividends, interest, and rents. Dividends, interest, and rents from community property are community income and must be evenly split. Dividends, interest, and rents from separate property are characterized in accordance with the discussion under *Income from separate property*, later.

Alimony received. Alimony or separate maintenance payments made prior to divorce are taxable to the payee spouse only to the extent they exceed 50% (his or her share) of the reportable community income. This is so because the payee spouse is already required to report half of the community income. See also *Alimony paid*, later.

Gains and losses. Gains and losses are classified as separate or community depending on how the property is held. For example, a loss on separate property, such as stock held separately, is a separate loss. On the other hand, a loss on community property, such as a casualty loss to your home held as community property, is a community loss. See Publication 544, Sales and Other Dispositions of Assets, for information on gains and losses. See Publication 547, Casualties, Disasters, and Thefts, for information on losses due to a casualty or theft.

Withdrawals from individual retirement arrangements (IRAs) and Coverdell Education Savings Accounts (ESAs). There are several kinds of individual retirement arrangements (IRAs). They are traditional IRAs (including SEP-IRAs), SIMPLE IRAs, and Roth IRAs. IRAs and ESAs by law are deemed to be separate property. Therefore, taxable IRA and ESA distributions are separate property, even if the funds in the account would otherwise be community property. These distributions are wholly taxable to the spouse (or RDP/California same-sex spouse) whose name is on the account. That spouse (or RDP/California same-sex spouse) is also liable for any penalties and additional taxes on the distributions.

Pensions. Generally, distributions from pensions will be characterized as community or separate income depending on the respective periods of participation in the pension while married (or during the registered domestic partnership/same-sex marriage in California) and domiciled in a community property state or in a noncommunity property state during the total period of participation in the pension. See the example under *Civil service retirement*, later. These rules may vary between states. Check your state law.

Lump-sum distributions. If you were born before January 2, 1936, and receive a lump-sum distribution from a qualified retirement plan, you may be able to choose an optional method of figuring the tax on the distribution. For the 10-year tax option, you must disregard community property laws. For more information, see Publication 575, Pension and Annuity Income, and Form 4972, Tax on Lump-Sum Distributions.

Civil service retirement. For income tax purposes, community property laws apply to annuities payable under the Civil Service Retirement Act (CSRS) or Federal Employee Retirement System (FERS).

Whether a civil service annuity is separate or community income depends on your marital status (or your status

Publication 555 (December 2010)

as a RDP/California same-sex spouse) and domicile of the employee when the services were performed for which the annuity is paid. Even if you now live in a noncommunity property state and you receive a civil service annuity, it may be community income if it is based on services you performed while married (or during the registered domestic partnership/same-sex marriage in California) and domiciled in a community property state.

If a civil service annuity is a mixture of community income and separate income, it must be divided between the two kinds of income. The division is based on the employee's domicile and marital status (or RDP/California same-sex marital status) in community and noncommunity property states during his or her periods of service.

Example. Henry Wright retired this year after 30 years of civil service. He and his wife were domiciled in a community property state during the past 15 years.

Since half the service was performed while the Wrights were married and domiciled in a community property state, half the civil service retirement pay is considered to be community income. If Mr. Wright receives $1,000 a month in retirement pay, $500 is considered community income—half ($250) is his income and half ($250) is his wife's.

Military retirement pay. State community property laws apply to military retirement pay. Generally, the pay is either separate or community income based on the marital status and domicile of the couple while the member of the Armed Forces was in active military service. For example, military retirement pay for services performed during marriage and domicile in a community property state is community income.

Active military pay earned while married and domiciled in a community property state is also community income. This income is considered to be received half by the member of the Armed Forces and half by the spouse.

Partnership income. If an interest is held in a partnership, and income from the partnership is attributable to the efforts of either spouse (or RDP/California same-sex spouse), the partnership income is community property. If it is merely a passive investment in a separate property partnership, the partnership income will be characterized in accordance with the discussion under *Income from separate property*, later.

Tax-exempt income. For spouses, community income exempt from federal tax generally keeps its exempt status for both spouses. For example, under certain circumstances, income earned outside the United States is tax exempt. If you earned income and met the conditions that made it exempt, the income is also exempt for your spouse even though he or she may not have met the conditions. RDPs and same-sex married couples in California should consult the particular exclusion provision to see if the exempt status applies to both.

Income from separate property. In some states, income from separate property is separate income. These states include Washington, Nevada, California, Arizona, and New Mexico. Other states characterize income from separate

property as community income. These states include Idaho, Louisiana, Wisconsin, and Texas.

Exemptions

When you file separate returns, you must claim your own exemption amount for that year. (See your tax return instructions.)

You cannot divide the amount allowed as an exemption for a dependent between you and your spouse (or RDP/California same-sex spouse). When community funds provide support for more than one person, each of whom otherwise qualifies as a dependent, you and your spouse (or RDP/California same-sex spouse) may divide the number of dependency exemptions as explained in the following example.

Example. Ron and Diane White have three dependent children and live in Nevada. If Ron and Diane file separately, only Ron can claim his own exemption, and only Diane can claim her own exemption. Ron and Diane can agree that one of them will claim the exemption for one, two, or all of their children and the other will claim any remaining exemptions. They cannot each claim half of the total exemption amount for their three children.

Deductions

If you file separate returns, your deductions generally depend on whether the expenses involve community or separate income.

Business and investment expenses. If you file separate returns, expenses incurred to earn or produce:

- Community business or investment income are generally divided equally between you and your spouse (or RDP/California same-sex spouse). Each of you is entitled to deduct one-half of the expenses on your separate returns.

- Separate business or investment income are deductible by the spouse (RDP/California same-sex spouse) who earns the income.

Other limits may also apply to business and investment expenses. For more information, see Publication 535, Business Expenses, and Publication 550, Investment Income and Expenses.

Alimony paid. Payments that may otherwise qualify as alimony are not deductible by the payer if they are the recipient spouse's part of community income. They are deductible as alimony only to the extent they are more than that spouse's part of community income.

Example. You live in a community property state. You are separated but the special rules explained later under *Spouses living apart all year* do not apply. Under a written agreement, you pay your spouse $12,000 of your $20,000 total yearly community income. Your spouse receives no other community income. Under your state law, earnings of a spouse living separately and apart from the other spouse continue as community property.

On your separate returns, each of you must report $10,000 of the total community income. In addition, your spouse must report $2,000 as alimony received. You can deduct $2,000 as alimony paid.

IRA deduction. Deductions for IRA contributions cannot be split between spouses (or RDPs/California same-sex spouses). The deduction for each spouse (or RDP/California same-sex spouse) is figured separately and without regard to community property laws.

Personal expenses. Expenses that are paid out of separate funds, such as medical expenses, are deductible by the spouse (or RDP/California same-sex spouse) who pays them. If these expenses are paid from community funds, divide the deduction equally between you and your spouse (or RDP/California same-sex spouse).

Credits, Taxes, and Payments

The following is a discussion of the general effect of community property laws on the treatment of certain credits, taxes, and payments on your separate return.

Child tax credit. You may be entitled to a child tax credit for each of your qualifying children. You must provide the name and identification number (usually the social security number) of each qualifying child on your return. See your tax package instructions for the maximum amount of the credit you can claim for each qualifying child.

Limit on credit. The credit is limited if your modified adjusted gross income (modified AGI) is above a certain amount. The amount at which the limitation (phaseout) begins depends on your filing status. Generally, your credit is limited to your tax liability unless you have three or more qualifying children. See your tax return instructions for more information.

Self-employment tax. This section discusses the effect of community property laws on the imposition of self-employment tax on the earnings and profits of a sole proprietorship and partnerships. For the effect of community property laws on the income tax treatment of income from a sole proprietorship and partnerships, see *Wages, earnings, and profits* and *Partnership income*, earlier. The following rules only apply to persons married for federal tax purposes. RDPs and same-sex spouses in California report community income for self-employment tax purposes the same way they do for income tax purposes.

Sole proprietorship. With regard to net income from a trade or business (other than a partnership) that is community income, self-employment tax is imposed on the spouse carrying on the trade or business.

Partnerships. All of the distributive share of a married partner's income or loss from a partnership trade or business is attributable to the partner for computing any self-employment tax, even if a portion of the partner's distributive share of income or loss is community income or loss that is otherwise attributable to the partner's spouse for income tax purposes. If both spouses are partners, any self-employment tax is allocated based on their distributive shares.

Federal income tax withheld. Report the credit for federal income tax withheld on community wages in the same manner as your wages. If you and your spouse file separate returns on which each of you reports half the community wages, each of you is entitled to credit for half the income tax withheld on those wages. Likewise, each RDP/California same-sex spouse is entitled to credit for half the income tax withheld on those wages.

Estimated tax payments. In determining whether you must pay estimated tax, apply the estimated tax rules to your estimated income. These rules are explained in Publication 505.

If you think you may owe estimated tax and want to pay the tax separately (RDPs and same-sex spouses in California must pay the tax separately), determine whether you must pay it by taking into account:

1. Half the community income and deductions,

2. All of your separate income and deductions, and

3. Your own exemption and any exemptions for dependents that you may claim.

Whether you and your spouse pay estimated tax jointly or separately will not affect your choice of filing joint or separate income tax returns.

If you and your spouse paid estimated tax jointly but file separate income tax returns, either of you can claim all of the estimated tax paid, or you may divide it between you in any way that you agree upon.

If you cannot agree on how to divide it, the estimated tax you can claim equals the total estimated tax paid times the tax shown on your separate return, divided by the total of the tax shown on your return and your spouse's return.

If you paid your estimated taxes separately, you get credit for only the estimated taxes you paid.

Earned income credit. You may be entitled to an earned income credit (EIC). You cannot claim this credit if your filing status is married filing separately.

If you are married, but qualify to file as head of household under rules for married taxpayers living apart (see Publication 501, Exemptions, Standard Deduction, and Filing Information), and live in a state that has community property laws, your earned income for the EIC does not include any amount earned by your spouse that is treated as belonging to you under community property laws. That amount is not earned income for the EIC, even though you must include it in your gross income on your income tax return. Your earned income includes the entire amount **you** earned, even if part of it is treated as belonging to your spouse under your state's community property laws. The same rule applies to RDPs and same-sex spouses in California.

 This rule does not apply when determining your adjusted gross income (AGI) for the EIC. Your AGI includes that part of both your and your spouse's (or RDP's/California same-sex spouse's) wages that you are required to include in gross income shown on your tax return.

For more information about the EIC, see Publication 596, Earned Income Credit (EIC).

Overpayments. The amount of an overpayment on a joint return is allocated under the community property laws of the state in which you are domiciled.

- If, under the laws of your state, community property is subject to premarital or other separate debts of either spouse, the full joint overpayment may be used to offset the obligation.

- If, under the laws of your state, community property is not subject to premarital or other separate debts of either spouse, only the portion of the joint overpayment allocated to the spouse liable for the obligation can be used to offset that liability. The portion allocated to the other spouse can be refunded.

Community Property Laws Disregarded

The following discussions are situations where special rules apply to community property and community income for spouses. These rules do not apply to RDPs (or California same-sex spouses).

Certain community income not treated as community income by one spouse. Community property laws may not apply to an item of community income that you received but did not treat as community income. You are responsible for reporting all of that income item if:

1. You treat the item as if only you are entitled to the income, and

2. You do not notify your spouse of the nature and amount of the income by the due date for filing the return (including extensions).

Relief from liability arising from community property law. You are not responsible for the tax relating to an item of community income if all the following conditions exist.

1. You did not file a joint return for the tax year.

2. You did not include an item of community income in gross income.

3. The item of community income you did not include is one of the following:

   a. Wages, salaries, and other compensation your spouse (or former spouse) received for services he or she performed as an employee.

   b. Income your spouse (or former spouse) derived from a trade or business he or she operated as a sole proprietor.

   c. Your spouse's (or former spouse's) distributive share of partnership income.

   d. Income from your spouse's (or former spouse's) separate property (other than income described in (a), (b), or (c)). Use the appropriate community property law to determine what is separate property.

e. Any other income that belongs to your spouse (or former spouse) under community property law.

4. You establish that you did not know of, and had no reason to know of, that community income.

5. Under all facts and circumstances, it would not be fair to include the item of community income in your gross income.

Requesting relief. For information on how and when to request relief from liabilities arising from community property laws, see *Community Property Laws* in Publication 971, Innocent Spouse Relief.

Equitable relief. If you do not qualify for the relief discussed earlier under *Relief from liability arising from community property law* and are now liable for an underpaid or understated tax you believe should be paid only by your spouse (or former spouse), you may request equitable relief. To request equitable relief, you must file Form 8857, Request for Innocent Spouse Relief. Also see Publication 971.

Spousal agreements. In some states a husband and wife may enter into an agreement that affects the status of property or income as community or separate property. Check your state law to determine how it affects you.

Nonresident alien spouse. If you are a United States citizen or resident alien and you choose to treat your nonresident alien spouse as a U.S. resident for tax purposes and you are domiciled in a community property state or country, use the community property rules. You must file a joint return for the year you make the choice. You can file separate returns in later years. For details on making this choice, see Publication 519, U.S. Tax Guide for Aliens.

If you are a U.S. citizen or resident alien and do not choose to treat your nonresident alien spouse as a U.S. resident for tax purposes, treat your community income as explained next under *Spouses living apart all year*. However, you do not have to meet the four conditions discussed there.

Spouses living apart all year. If you are married at any time during the calendar year, special rules apply for reporting certain community income. You must meet all the following conditions for these special rules to apply.

1. You and your spouse lived apart all year.

2. You and your spouse did not file a joint return for a tax year beginning or ending in the calendar year.

3. You and/or your spouse had earned income for the calendar year that is community income.

4. You and your spouse have not transferred, directly or indirectly, any of the earned income in condition (3) above between yourselves before the end of the year. Do not take into account transfers satisfying child support obligations or transfers of very small amounts or value.

If all these conditions are met, you and your spouse must report your community income as discussed next. See also

Certain community income not treated as community income by one spouse, earlier.

Earned income. Treat earned income that is not trade or business or partnership income as the income of the spouse who performed the services to earn the income. Earned income is wages, salaries, professional fees, and other pay for personal services.

Earned income does not include amounts paid by a corporation that are a distribution of earnings and profits rather than a reasonable allowance for personal services rendered.

Trade or business income. Treat income and related deductions from a trade or business that is not a partnership as those of the spouse carrying on the trade or business.

Partnership income or loss. Treat income or loss from a trade or business carried on by a partnership as the income or loss of the spouse who is the partner.

Separate property income. Treat income from the separate property of one spouse as the income of that spouse.

Social security benefits. Treat social security and equivalent railroad retirement benefits as the income of the spouse who receives the benefits.

Other income. Treat all other community income, such as dividends, interest, rents, royalties, or gains, as provided under your state's community property law.

Example. George and Sharon were married throughout the year but did not live together at any time during the year. Both domiciles were in a community property state. They did not file a joint return or transfer any of their earned income between themselves. During the year their incomes were as follows:

	George	Sharon
Wages	$20,000	$22,000
Consulting business	5,000	
Partnership		10,000
Dividends from separate property	1,000	2,000
Interest from community property	500	500
Total	$26,500	$34,500

Under the community property law of their state, all the income is considered community income. (Some states treat income from separate property as separate income— check your state law.) Sharon did not take part in George's consulting business.

Ordinarily, on their separate returns they would each report $30,500, half the total community income of $61,000 ($26,500 + $34,500). But because they meet the four conditions listed earlier under *Spouses living apart all year*, they must disregard community property law in reporting all their income (except the interest income) from community property. They each report on their returns only their own earnings and other income, and their share of the interest income from community property. George reports $26,500 and Sharon reports $34,500.

Other separated spouses. If you and your spouse are separated but do not meet the four conditions discussed

earlier under *Spouses living apart all year*, you must treat your income according to the laws of your state. In some states, income earned after separation but before a decree of divorce continues to be community income. In other states it is separate income.

End of the Community

The marital community may end in several ways. When the marital community ends, the community assets (money and property) are divided between the spouses. Similarly, a same-sex couple's community may end in several ways and the community assets must be divided between the RDPs or California same-sex spouses.

Death of spouse. If you own community property and your spouse dies, the total fair market value (FMV) of the community property, including the part that belongs to you, generally becomes the basis of the entire property. For this rule to apply, at least half the value of the community property interest must be includible in your spouse's gross estate, whether or not the estate must file a return (this rule does not apply to RDPs and individuals married to a same-sex spouse in California).

For example, Bob and Ann owned community property that had a basis of $80,000. When Bob died, his and Ann's community property had an FMV of $100,000. One-half of the FMV of their community interest was includible in Bob's estate. The basis of Ann's half of the property is $50,000 after Bob died (half of the $100,000 FMV). The basis of the other half to Bob's heirs is also $50,000.

For more information about the basis of assets, see Publication 551, Basis of Assets.

 The above basis rule does not apply if your spouse died in 2010 and the spouse's executor elected out of the estate tax, in which case section 1022 will apply. See Publication 4895, Tax Treatment of Property Acquired From a Decedent Dying in 2010, for additional information.

Divorce or separation. If spouses divorce or separate, the (equal or unequal) division of community property in connection with the divorce or property settlement does not result in a gain or loss (this rule does not apply to RDPs or same-sex married couples in California). For information on the tax consequences of the division of property under a property settlement or divorce decree, see Publication 504.

Each spouse (or RDP/California same-sex spouse) is taxed on half the community income for the part of the year before the community ends. However, see *Spouses living apart all year*, earlier. Any income received after the community ends is separate income. This separate income is taxable only to the spouse (or RDP/California same-sex spouse) to whom it belongs.

An **absolute decree of divorce or annulment** ends the marital community in all community property states. A decree of annulment, even though it holds that no valid marriage ever existed, usually does not nullify community property rights arising during the "marriage." However, you should check your state law for exceptions.

Publication 555 (December 2010)

A *decree of legal separation or of separate maintenance* may or may not end the marital community. The court issuing the decree may terminate the marital community and divide the property between the spouses.

A *separation agreement* may divide the community property between you and your spouse. It may provide that this property, along with future earnings and property acquired, will be separate property. This agreement may end the community.

In some states, the marital community ends when the spouses permanently separate, even if there is no formal agreement. Check your state law.

If you are an RDP or an individual married to a same-sex individual in California, you should check your state law to determine when the community ends.

Preparing a Federal Income Tax Return

The following discussion does not apply to spouses who meet the conditions under *Spouses living apart all year*, discussed earlier. Those spouses must report their community income as explained in that discussion.

Joint Return Versus Separate Returns

Ordinarily, filing a joint return will give you a greater tax advantage than filing a separate return. But in some cases, your combined income tax on separate returns may be less than it would be on a joint return.

The following rules apply if your filing status is married filing separately.

1. You should itemize deductions if your spouse itemizes deductions, because you cannot claim the standard deduction,

2. You cannot take the credit for child and dependent care expenses in most instances,

3. You cannot take the earned income credit,

4. You cannot exclude any interest income from qualified U.S. savings bonds that you used for higher education expenses,

5. You cannot take the credit for the elderly or the disabled unless you lived apart from your spouse all year,

6. You may have to include in income more of any social security benefits (including any equivalent railroad retirement benefits) you received during the year than you would on a joint return,

7. You cannot deduct interest paid on a qualified student loan,

8. You cannot take the education credits,

9. You may have a smaller child tax credit than you would on a joint return, and

10. You cannot take the exclusion or credit for adoption expenses in most instances.

 Figure your tax both on a joint return and on separate returns under the community property laws of your state. You can then compare the tax figured under both methods and use the one that results in less tax.

Separate Return Preparation

If you file separate returns, you and your spouse must each report half of your combined community income and deductions in addition to your separate income and deductions. List only your share of the income and deductions on the appropriate lines of your separate tax returns (wages, interest, dividends, etc.). The same reporting rule applies to RDPs and individuals in California who are married to an individual of the same sex. For a discussion of the effect of community property laws on certain items of income, deductions, credits, and other return amounts, see *Identifying Income, Deductions, and Credits*, earlier.

Attach a worksheet to your separate returns showing how you figured the income, deductions, and federal income tax withheld that each of you reported. The *Allocation Worksheet* (Table 2) shown later can be used for this purpose. If you are a RDP or an individual in California married to an individual of the same sex, you may want to write the social security number of your partner or same-sex spouse in the "Notes" section of the worksheet to avoid delays in the processing of your return. If you do not attach a worksheet, you and your spouse (or RDP/California same-sex spouse) should each attach a photocopy of the other spouse's (or RDP's/California same-sex spouse's) Form W-2, Wage and Tax Statement, or 1099-R, Distributions From Pensions, Retirement or Profit-Sharing Plans, IRAs, Insurance Contracts, etc. Make a notation on the form showing the division of income and tax withheld.

Extension of time to file. An extension of time for filing your separate return does not extend the time for filing your spouse's (or RDP's/California same-sex spouse's) separate return. If you and your spouse file a joint return, you cannot file separate returns after the due date for filing either separate return has passed.

Table 2. **Allocation Worksheet**

	1 Total Income (Community/Separate)	2 Allocated to Spouse, RDP, or California Same-Sex Spouse #1	3 Allocated to Spouse, RDP, or California Same-Sex Spouse #2
1. Wages (each employer)			
2. Interest Income (each payer)			
3. Dividends (each payer)			
4. State Income Tax Refund			
5. Capital Gains and Losses			
6. Pension Income			
7. Rents, Royalties, Partnerships, Estates, Trusts			
8. Taxes Withheld			
9. Other items such as: Social Security Benefits, Business and Farm Income or Loss, Unemployment Compensation, Mortgage Interest Deduction, etc.			

NOTES

_____

_____

_____

_____

_____

Publication 555 (December 2010)

Example

Walter and Mary Smith are married and domiciled in a community property state. Their two children (18-year-old twins) and Mary's mother live with them and qualify as their dependents. Amounts paid for their support were paid out of community funds.

Walter received a salary of $53,424. Income tax withheld from his salary was $4,704. Walter received $132 in taxable interest from his savings account. He also received $217 in dividends from stock that he owned. His interest and dividend income are his separate income under the laws of his community property state.

Mary received $200 in dividends from stock that she owned. This is her separate income. In addition, she received $4,200 as a part-time dental technician. No income tax was withheld from her salary.

The Smiths paid a total of $5,775 in medical expenses. Medical insurance of $1,050 was paid out of community funds. Walter paid $4,725 out of his separate funds for an operation he had.

The Smiths had $10,264 in other itemized deductions, none of which were miscellaneous itemized deductions subject to the 2%-of-adjusted-gross-income limit. The amounts spent for these deductions were paid out of community funds.

To see if it is to the Smiths' advantage to file a joint return or separate returns, a worksheet (Table 3, shown next) is prepared to figure their federal income tax both ways. Walter and Mary must claim their own exemptions on their separate returns.

The summary at the bottom of the worksheet compares the tax figured on the Smiths' joint return to the total tax figured by adding the tax amounts on their separate returns. By filing separately under the community property laws of their state, the Smiths save $243 in income tax.

If the Smiths were domiciled in Idaho, Louisiana, Texas, or Wisconsin, the result would be slightly different because in those states income from separate property generally is treated as community income. If they lived in one of those states, the interest from Walter's savings account and the dividends from stock owned by each of them would be divided equally on their separate returns.

 In figuring your tax, use the amounts from your current tax forms instruction booklet for items such as the standard deduction, exemption allowance, and Tax Table tax. The amounts used in this example apply for 2010 only. The example shows how filing separate returns under community property tax laws can result in lower tax than filing jointly; you must figure your own tax both ways to know which works better for you.

Table 3. **Worksheet — Walter and Mary Smith**

	Joint Return	Separate Returns	
		Walter's	Mary's
Income (Walter's):			
Salary...................................	$ 53,424	$ 26,712	$ 26,712
Interest and dividends ($217 dividends + $132 interest)	349	349	–0–
Total	$ 53,773	$ 27,061	$ 26,712
Income (Mary's):			
Salary...................................	$ 4,200	$ 2,100	$ 2,100
Dividends	200	–0–	200
Total	4,400	2,100	2,300
Adjusted gross income (AGI)	$ 58,173	$ 29,161	$ 29,012
Deductions:			
Community: (Not subject to the 2% AGI limit)	$ 10,264	$ 5,132	$ 5,132
Medical:			
Premiums...........................	$ 1,050	$ 525	$ 525
Medical expenses (Walter's)	4,725	4,725	–0–
Total..............................	$ 5,775	$ 5,250	$ 525
(Minus) 7.5% of AGI	(4,363)	(2,187)	(2,176)
Medical expense deduction	$ 1,412	$ 3,063	$ –0–
Total deductions	$ 11,676	$ 8,195	$ 5,132
Subtract total deductions from AGI[1,2]	$ 46,497	$ 20,966	$ 23,880
Exemptions[1,3](Subtract to find taxable income)	$(18,250)	$ (7,300)	$ (10,950)
Taxable Income	$ 28,247	$ 13,666	$ 12,930
Tax[1,4]	$ 3,396	$ 1,633	$ 1,520
Federal income tax withheld	$ 4,704	$ 2,352	$ 2,352
Overpayment (Subtract from Federal tax withheld)	$ 1,308	$ 719	$ 832

[1] **Caution:** In figuring your tax, use the amounts from your current tax forms instruction booklet for such items as the standard deduction, exemption allowance, and Tax Table tax.

[2] The itemized deductions are greater than the standard deduction (shown here as $11,400 for married filing jointly and $5,700 for married filing separately). **Note:** If one spouse itemizes, the other must itemize, even if one spouse's deductions are less than the standard deduction.

[3] An allowance of $3,650 for each exemption claimed is subtracted — 5 on the joint return, 2 on Walter's separate return, and 3 on Mary's separate return.

[4] The tax on the joint return is from the column of the 2010 Tax Table for married filing jointly. The tax on Walter's and Mary's separate returns is from the column of the 2010 Tax Table for married filing separately.

Table 3. **Summary**

Tax on joint return...............		$ 3,396
Tax on Walter's separate return	$ 1,633	
Tax on Mary's separate return	1,520	
Total tax filing separate returns		$3,153
Total savings by filing separate returns		$243

Publication 555 (December 2010)

How To Get Tax Help

You can get help with unresolved tax issues, order free publications and forms, ask tax questions, and get information from the IRS in several ways. By selecting the method that is best for you, you will have quick and easy access to tax help.

Contacting your Taxpayer Advocate. The Taxpayer Advocate Service (TAS) is an independent organization within the IRS. We help taxpayers who are experiencing economic harm, such as not being able to provide necessities like housing, transportation, or food; taxpayers who are seeking help in resolving tax problems with the IRS; and those who believe that an IRS system or procedure is not working as it should. Here are seven things every taxpayer should know about TAS:

- The Taxpayer Advocate Service is your voice at the IRS.

- Our service is free, confidential, and tailored to meet your needs.

- You may be eligible for our help if you have tried to resolve your tax problem through normal IRS channels and have gotten nowhere, or you believe an IRS procedure just isn't working as it should.

- We help taxpayers whose problems are causing financial difficulty or significant cost, including the cost of professional representation. This includes businesses as well as individuals.

- Our employees know the IRS and how to navigate it. If you qualify for our help, we'll assign your case to an advocate who will listen to your problem, help you understand what needs to be done to resolve it, and stay with you every step of the way until your problem is resolved.

- We have at least one local taxpayer advocate in every state, the District of Columbia, and Puerto Rico. You can call your local advocate, whose number is in your phone book, in Pub. 1546, Taxpayer Advocate Service—Your Voice at the IRS, and on our website at *www.irs.gov/advocate*. You can also call our toll-free line at 1-877-777-4778 or TTY/TDD 1-800-829-4059.

- You can learn about your rights and responsibilities as a taxpayer by visiting our online tax toolkit at *www.taxtoolkit.irs.gov*. You can get updates on hot tax topics by visiting our YouTube channel at *www.youtube.com/tasnta* and our Facebook page at *www.facebook.com/YourVoiceAtIRS*, or by following our tweets at *www.twitter.com/YourVoiceAtIRS*.

Low Income Taxpayer Clinics (LITCs). The Low Income Taxpayer Clinic program serves individuals who have a problem with the IRS and whose income is below a certain level. LITCs are independent from the IRS. Most LITCs can provide representation before the IRS or in court on audits, tax collection disputes, and other issues for free or a small fee. If an individual's native language is not English, some clinics can provide multilingual information about taxpayer rights and responsibilities. For more information, see Publication 4134, Low Income Taxpayer Clinic List. This publication is available at IRS.gov, by calling 1-800-TAX-FORM (1-800-829-3676), or at your local IRS office.

Free tax services. Publication 910, IRS Guide to Free Tax Services, is your guide to IRS services and resources. Learn about free tax information from the IRS, including publications, services, and education and assistance programs. The publication also has an index of over 100 TeleTax topics (recorded tax information) you can listen to on the telephone. The majority of the information and services listed in this publication are available to you free of charge. If there is a fee associated with a resource or service, it is listed in the publication.

Accessible versions of IRS published products are available on request in a variety of alternative formats for people with disabilities.

Free help with your return. Free help in preparing your return is available nationwide from IRS-trained volunteers. The Volunteer Income Tax Assistance (VITA) program is designed to help low-income taxpayers and the Tax Counseling for the Elderly (TCE) program is designed to assist taxpayers age 60 and older with their tax returns. Many VITA sites offer free electronic filing and all volunteers will let you know about credits and deductions you may be entitled to claim. To find the nearest VITA or TCE site, call 1-800-829-1040.

As part of the TCE program, AARP offers the Tax-Aide counseling program. To find the nearest AARP Tax-Aide site, call 1-888-227-7669 or visit AARP's website at *www.aarp.org/money/taxaide*.

For more information on these programs, go to IRS.gov and enter keyword "VITA" in the upper right-hand corner.

 Internet. You can access the IRS website at IRS.gov 24 hours a day, 7 days a week to:

- *E-file* your return. Find out about commercial tax preparation and *e-file* services available free to eligible taxpayers.

- Check the status of your 2010 refund. Go to IRS.gov and click on *Where's My Refund*. Wait at least 72 hours after the IRS acknowledges receipt of your e-filed return, or 3 to 4 weeks after mailing a paper return. If you filed Form 8379 with your return, wait 14 weeks (11 weeks if you filed electronically). Have your 2010 tax return available so you can provide your social security number, your filing status, and the exact whole dollar amount of your refund.

- Download forms, including talking tax forms, instructions, and publications.

- Order IRS products online.

- Research your tax questions online.

- Search publications online by topic or keyword.

- Use the online Internal Revenue Code, regulations, or other official guidance.

- View Internal Revenue Bulletins (IRBs) published in the last few years.
- Figure your withholding allowances using the withholding calculator online at *www.irs.gov/individuals*.
- Determine if Form 6251 must be filed by using our Alternative Minimum Tax (AMT) Assistant.
- Sign up to receive local and national tax news by email.
- Get information on starting and operating a small business.

 Phone. Many services are available by phone.

- *Ordering forms, instructions, and publications.* Call 1-800-TAX-FORM (1-800-829-3676) to order current-year forms, instructions, and publications, and prior-year forms and instructions. You should receive your order within 10 days.
- *Asking tax questions.* Call the IRS with your tax questions at 1-800-829-1040.
- *Solving problems.* You can get face-to-face help solving tax problems every business day in IRS Taxpayer Assistance Centers. An employee can explain IRS letters, request adjustments to your account, or help you set up a payment plan. Call your local Taxpayer Assistance Center for an appointment. To find the number, go to *www.irs.gov/localcontacts* or look in the phone book under *United States Government, Internal Revenue Service*.
- *TTY/TDD equipment.* If you have access to TTY/TDD equipment, call 1-800-829-4059 to ask tax questions or to order forms and publications.
- *TeleTax topics.* Call 1-800-829-4477 to listen to pre-recorded messages covering various tax topics.
- *Refund information.* To check the status of your 2010 refund, call 1-800-829-1954 or 1-800-829-4477 (automated refund information 24 hours a day, 7 days a week). Wait at least 72 hours after the IRS acknowledges receipt of your e-filed return, or 3 to 4 weeks after mailing a paper return. If you filed Form 8379 with your return, wait 14 weeks (11 weeks if you filed electronically). Have your 2010 tax return available so you can provide your social security number, your filing status, and the exact whole dollar amount of your refund. If you check the status of your refund and are not given the date it will be issued, please wait until the next week before checking back.
- *Other refund information.* To check the status of a prior-year refund or amended return refund, call 1-800-829-1040.

Evaluating the quality of our telephone services. To ensure IRS representatives give accurate, courteous, and professional answers, we use several methods to evaluate the quality of our telephone services. One method is for a second IRS representative to listen in on or record random telephone calls. Another is to ask some callers to complete a short survey at the end of the call.

 Walk-in. Many products and services are available on a walk-in basis.

- *Products.* You can walk in to many post offices, libraries, and IRS offices to pick up certain forms, instructions, and publications. Some IRS offices, libraries, grocery stores, copy centers, city and county government offices, credit unions, and office supply stores have a collection of products available to print from a CD or photocopy from reproducible proofs. Also, some IRS offices and libraries have the Internal Revenue Code, regulations, Internal Revenue Bulletins, and Cumulative Bulletins available for research purposes.
- *Services.* You can walk in to your local Taxpayer Assistance Center every business day for personal, face-to-face tax help. An employee can explain IRS letters, request adjustments to your tax account, or help you set up a payment plan. If you need to resolve a tax problem, have questions about how the tax law applies to your individual tax return, or you are more comfortable talking with someone in person, visit your local Taxpayer Assistance Center where you can spread out your records and talk with an IRS representative face-to-face. No appointment is necessary—just walk in. If you prefer, you can call your local Center and leave a message requesting an appointment to resolve a tax account issue. A representative will call you back within 2 business days to schedule an in-person appointment at your convenience. If you have an ongoing, complex tax account problem or a special need, such as a disability, an appointment can be requested. All other issues will be handled without an appointment. To find the number of your local office, go to *www.irs.gov/localcontacts* or look in the phone book under *United States Government, Internal Revenue Service*.

 Mail. You can send your order for forms, instructions, and publications to the address below. You should receive a response within 10 days after your request is received.

Internal Revenue Service
1201 N. Mitsubishi Motorway
Bloomington, IL 61705-6613

 DVD for tax products. You can order Publication 1796, IRS Tax Products DVD, and obtain:

- Current-year forms, instructions, and publications.
- Prior-year forms, instructions, and publications.
- Tax Map: an electronic research tool and finding aid.

Publication 555 (December 2010)

- Tax law frequently asked questions.
- Tax Topics from the IRS telephone response system.
- Internal Revenue Code—Title 26 of the U.S. Code.
- Fill-in, print, and save features for most tax forms.
- Internal Revenue Bulletins.
- Toll-free and email technical support.
- Two releases during the year.
  - The first release will ship the beginning of January 2011.
  - The final release will ship the beginning of March 2011.

Purchase the DVD from National Technical Information Service (NTIS) at *www.irs.gov/cdorders* for $30 (no handling fee) or call 1-877-233-6767 toll free to buy the DVD for $30 (plus a $6 handling fee).

Index

Appendix C - CP/SP Worksheet

CP/SP Worksheet

Use this worksheet to document all of your property and its CP/SP character

Partner 1 = _____

Partner 2 = _____

Date of Registration as Washington SRDPs _____

List/Description of Property	CP	SP Ptr 1	SP Ptr 2	Notes

Additional Notes:

Appendix D – Sample Attachments for RDP Returns

Sample Cover Sheet

California Registered Domestic Partner or Same-Sex Married Couple Special Handling Required

This tax return has been prepared in accordance with CCA 201021050 to split income from community property between the following two California State registered domestic partners.

Partner 1 Name – Partner 1 Social Security Number

Partner 2 Name – Partner 2 Social Security Number

The taxpayers are California Registered Domestic Partners/Same-Sex Married Couple and are required to file their tax returns in compliance with CCA 201021050.

These returns are being filed to allocate the community property income between the taxpayers. Income from separate property income has been reported 100% on the tax return of the owner of the separate property.

W-2 wages have been split between the taxpayers by first showing 100% on Line 7 of the earning taxpayer and then adjusting on Line 21 for one-half of the wages.

Federal tax withholding from W-2s has been split between the taxpayers on Form 1040, line 61.

Estimated tax payments, if any, have been allocated 100% to the taxpayer making the payment.

Attachments included are:

A summary of the allocation of tax withholding

A worksheet detailing the allocation of income and deduction between RDPs

Sample Federal Withholding Worksheet

Federal Withholding Allocation Worksheet
A Schedule to be Made Part of Form 1040
US Individual Income Tax Return
For Calendar Tax Year 2010

| | | | Claimed on Tax Return Per CCA 201021050 | |
| | Reported on Form W-2 | | | |
Taxpayer	SSN	Total	Bartok	Hobart
Bartok	111-11-1111	$ 60,000	$ 30,000	$ 30,000
Hobart	222-22-2222	15,000	7,500	7,500
Total		$ 75,000	$ 37,500	$ 37,500

Sample Pub 555 Worksheet

Example - Your Form will include different items based on your actual income/deductions for the year. Example assumes income/deductions are CP except for Other Income which is SP

Allocation of RDP Income and Deductions
A Schedule to be Made Part of Form 1040
US Individual Income Tax Return
For Calendar Tax Year 2010

		Allocated to	
	Total	TP 1	TP 2
Income:			
TP 1 Wages	$60,000	$30,000	$30,000
TP 2 Wages	40,000	20,000	20,000
TP 1 Interest	1,000	500	500
TP 2 Interest	200	100	100
TP 1 Dividends	50	25	25
TP 2 Dividends	50	25	25
TP 1 Other Income (TP 1's SP)	5,000	5,000	0
TP 2 Other Income	0	0	0
Adjusted Gross Income	$106,300	$55,650	$50,650
Itemized Deductions:			
Real Estate Taxes	$5,000	$2,500	$2,500
Taxes	20,000	10,000	10,000
Contributions	3,000	1,500	1,500
Total Itemized Deductions	$28,000	$14,000	$14,000

Appendix E – FTB Publication 737

STATE OF CALIFORNIA
FRANCHISE TAX BOARD

FTB Publication 737

Tax Information for Registered Domestic Partners

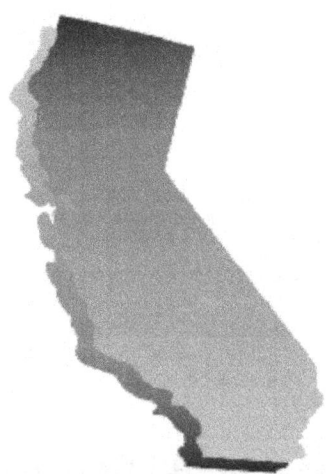

Contents

Purpose

This publication is primarily to assist registered domestic partners (RDPs) in filing their California income tax returns, if they have RDP adjustments. We have also included additional information about the history of RDP legislation and community property information that may be useful in completing the tax return.

The Internal Revenue Service (IRS) in a May 5, 2010, Chief Counsel Advice (CCA) memorandum stated that California RDPs must report one-half of their community income on his or her federal income tax return, unless the RDPs previously executed an agreement opting out of community property treatment. In a previous CCA, the IRS stated that an RDP had to report all of his or her earned income on his or her own federal tax return. This new CCA reverses that position.

The new CCA only addresses the treatment of community income of RDPs; it does not change the RDP's federal filing status. For federal purposes, an RDP will continue to use the single or head of household filing status.

RDP adjustments may be required on the California tax return because the filing status of an RDP for California purposes is not the same as the filing status that the RDP uses for federal purposes. Under California law, RDPs must file their California income tax returns using either the married/RDP filing jointly or married/RDP filing separately filing status. RDPs are not allowed to use a married filing status on their federal tax returns. Frequently, the dollar limits for a single taxpayer and a married couple are the same and the dollar limit for a married person filing separately is one-half the amount for a single person or a married couple. To apply the correct dollar limits on the California tax return, an RDP might be required to reduce the amount of a deduction reflected on a federal tax return.

Another category of adjustment occurs when the substantive rule for a transaction is different for a married person. For example, no gain or loss is recognized when spouses transfer property among themselves. Since an RDP is treated as a spouse for California purposes, no gain or loss is recognized for California purposes when one RDP transfers property to his or her domestic partner. However, this transfer is not likely to get the same treatment for federal purposes and gain or loss might be recognized for federal purposes.

INTERNET ASSISTANCE

Our website provides the information you need to complete your tax return. Go to **ftb.ca.gov** to:

- View your payments, balance due, wage and withholding information, and FTB-issued Forms 1099 on MyFTB Account.
- Pay your personal income taxes online using Web Pay. You choose the payment date, up to one year in advance.
- Download tax forms and publications.
- e-file your personal income tax return using CalFile.
- Check the status of your refund.
- Apply to make monthly payments using Installment Agreement Request.
- Access FTB legal notices, rulings, and regulations.
- Review FTB's analysis of pending legislation.
- Sign up to receive emails on a variety of tax topics through our Subscription Services.
- View internal procedure manuals to learn how we administer the law.

RDP adjustments include, but are not limited to the following:

- Division of community property
- Capital losses
- Transactions between RDPs
- Sale of residence
- Dependent care assistance
- Investment interest
- Qualified residence acquisition loan & equity loan interest
- Expense depreciation property limitations
- Individual Retirement Account
- Education loan interest
- Rental real estate passive loss
- Rollover of publicly traded securities gains into specialized small business investment companies

There are three possible methods to file if you are an RDP.

If you do not have any RDP adjustments:

1. Combine federal Form 1040, line 37 from each individual federal Form 1040 filed with the IRS and transfer the combined amount to Form 540, 540A, or 540NR (Long or Short), line 13.

   Note: RDPs who split their community income on their federal tax return and have no RDP adjustments may use this method.

If you have RDP adjustments, you will need to recalculate your federal adjusted gross income (AGI), before completing your California income tax return. You may use either one of the following methods:

2. Complete the California RDP Adjustments Worksheet (included in this publication).
3. Complete a pro forma federal Form 1040. A pro forma federal Form 1040 must be prepared using the same filing status used on your California tax return.

A pro forma federal Form 1040, is a federal tax return completed in the same manner that a married couple would report income and expenses.

The pro forma federal Form 1040 is used only to assist you in completing your California tax return. **DO NOT file the pro forma federal Form 1040 with the IRS.**

To complete the pro forma federal Form 1040 or the worksheet, follow the federal Form 1040 instructions along with the instructions provided in this publication.

General Information

In general, for taxable years beginning on or after January 1, 2010, California law conforms to the Internal Revenue Code (IRC) as of January 1, 2009. However, there are continuing differences between California and federal law. When California conforms to federal tax law changes, we do not always adopt all of the changes made at the federal level. For more information, go to **ftb.ca.gov** and search for **conformity**. Additional information can be found in FTB Pub. 1001, Supplemental Guidelines to California Adjustments, the instructions for California Schedule CA (540 or 540NR), and the Business Entity tax booklets.

The instructions provided with California tax forms are a summary of California tax law and are only intended to aid taxpayers in preparing their state income tax returns. We include information that is most useful to the greatest number of taxpayers in the limited space available. It is not possible to include all requirements of the California Revenue and Taxation Code (R&TC) in the tax booklets. Taxpayers should not consider the tax booklets as authoritative law.

In general, California affords the same rights and responsibilities to RDPs that previously were available only to married individuals. For California tax purposes, the same long-standing rules applicable to married individuals (relating to filing status, community property income, etc.) now apply to RDPs. However, because the federal government does not recognize domestic partners as married individuals for federal tax (IRS) purposes, RDPs must continue to file as unmarried individuals on their federal tax returns.

Under California law, RDPs must file their California income tax returns using either the married/RDP filing jointly or married/RDP filing separately filing status. RDPs will have the same legal benefits, protections, and responsibilities as married couples unless otherwise specified.

Substantially Equivalent – If you entered into a same-sex legal union in another state, other than a marriage, and that union has been determined to be substantially equivalent to a California registered domestic partnership, you are required to file a California income tax return using either the married/RDP filing jointly or married/RDP filing separately filing status.

For purposes of California income tax, references to a spouse, husband, or wife also refer to a California RDP, unless otherwise specified. When we use the initials RDP they refer to both a California registered domestic "partner" and a California registered domestic "partnership," as applicable.

California Registered Domestic Partners

California Family Code Section 297 provides that "domestic partners are two adults who have chosen to share one another's lives in an intimate and committed relationship of mutual caring."

Registered Domestic Partnership Requirements

A domestic partnership is established in California when both persons file a Declaration of Domestic Partnership with the California Secretary of State, and at the time of filing, all of the following requirements are met:

- Either of the following:

- ▶ Both persons are members of the same sex.
- ▶ One or both of the persons is/are over the age of 62 and meet the eligibility criteria under Title II of the Social Security Act as defined in 42 U.S.C. Section 402(a) for old-age insurance benefits or Title XVI of the Social Security Act as defined in 42 U.S.C. Section 1381 for aged individuals.
- Both persons have a common residence.
- Neither person is married to someone else or is a member of another domestic partnership with someone else that has not been terminated, dissolved, or adjudged a nullity.
- The two persons are not related by blood in a way that would prevent them from being married to each other in California.
- Both persons are at least 18 years of age.
- Both persons are capable of consenting to the domestic partnership.

The definition of "common residence" means that both domestic partners share the same residence. It is not necessary that the legal right to possess the common residence be in both of their names. Two people have a common residence even if one or both have additional residences. Domestic partners do not cease to have a common residence if one leaves the common residence but intends to return.

For additional domestic partner registration information, go to the California Secretary of State website at **sos.ca.gov** and search for **domestic partners registry** or call 916.653.3984.

Legislative History

Effective January 1, 2000, California legislation provided for the definition, registration, and termination of a domestic partner with the California Secretary of State. It also provided an option for state and local public employers to extend benefits to domestic partners under the Public Employees' Medical and Hospital Care Act and specified domestic hospital visitation rights.

Effective January 1, 2002, California legislation was

enacted that treated an RDP as a spouse of the taxpayer for certain medical tax benefits.

Effective January 1, 2005, rights, benefits, and privileges were added which treated RDPs the same as married persons, with the exception that they could not file a California income tax return using the married filing jointly or married filing separately filing status in the same manner as married persons. Included within those rights, benefits, and privileges were community property rights (with the exception of earned income) which were applied to a registered domestic partnership as of the date of registration. This changed with the passage of law effective January 1, 2007, which requires RDPs, beginning in 2007, to file their California income tax returns using the married/RDP filing jointly or married/RDP filing separately filing status. Also beginning in 2007, RDP's earned income is treated as community property. For more detailed information, go to **ftb.ca.gov** and search for **rdp** and view legislative history.

Attachments to Your Tax Return

Did you attach any federal forms or schedules other than Schedule A (Form 1040), Itemized Deductions, Schedule B (Form 1040), Interest and Ordinary Dividends, Schedule L (Form 1040), Standard Deduction for Certain Filers, or Schedule M (Form 1040), Making Work Pay Credit, to your federal Form 1040?

No Do not attach a copy of your federal Form 1040 return to Form 540.

Yes Attach a copy of both RDP's federal Forms 1040 filed with the IRS and all supporting federal forms and schedules to Form 540.

Note: Attach a copy of either the California RDP Adjustments Worksheet or federal pro forma Form 1040 if used to complete your Form 540.

If the tax software product you use prevents you from filing the required attachment(s), you should retain copies of all documentation which may be requested at a later date.

Do I Have to File a California Income Tax Return?

Filing Requirements for RDP Residents, Nonresidents, and Part-Year Residents

Residents – File a California tax return if either your gross income (which consists of all income you received from all sources in the form of money, goods, property, and services, that is not exempt from tax) or your adjusted gross income (which consists of your federal adjusted gross income from all sources, reduced or increased by all California income adjustments) is more than the amounts shown on the chart below for your filing status, age, and number of dependents.

Nonresidents and Part-Year Residents – File a California tax return if you have any income from California sources and your gross income (which consists of all income you received from all sources in the form of money, goods, property, and services, that is not exempt from tax) or adjusted gross income (which consists of your federal adjusted gross income from all sources, reduced or increased by all California income adjustments) is more than the amounts shown on the chart below for your filing status, age, and number of dependents.

Note: If your gross income or adjusted gross income is less than the amounts listed on the chart, you may still have a filing requirement. For more information, get California Form 540/540A Personal Income Tax Booklet or California Form 540NR Nonresident or Part-Year Resident Income Tax Booklet.

On 12/31/10, my filing status was:	and on 12/31/10, my age was: (If your 65th birthday is on January 1, 2011, you are considered to be age 65 on December 31, 2010)	California Gross Income			California Adjusted Gross Income		
		Dependents			Dependents		
		0	1	2 or more	0	1	2 or more
Head of household (Get FTB Pub.1540, California Head of Household Filing Status)	Under 65	14,754	18,054	20,529	11,803	15,103	17,578
	65 or older	19,704	22,179	24,159	16,753	19,228	21,208
Married/RDP filing jointly Married/RDP filing separately (The income of both spouses/RDPs must be combined; both spouses/RDPs may be required to file a tax return even if only one spouse/RDP had income over the amounts listed.)	Under 65 (both spouses/RDPs)	29,508	32,808	35,283	23,607	26,907	29,382
	65 or older (one spouse/RDP)	34,458	36,933	38,913	28,557	31,032	33,012
	65 or older (both spouses/RDPs)	39,408	41,883	43,863	33,507	35,982	37,962
Qualifying widow(er)	Under 65		18,054	20,529		15,103	17,578
	65 or older		22,179	24,159		19,228	21,208
Dependent of another person Any filing status	Any age	More than your standard deduction (Use the California Standard Deduction Worksheet for Dependents on page 9 to figure your standard deduction.)					

Filing Status

Note: If you are filing as an RDP, be sure to fill in the circle next to the question in the Filing Status section of the tax return that asks "If your California filing status is different from your federal status, fill in the circle here."

Married/RDP Filing Jointly – If **any** of the following is true:
- You were an RDP as of December 31, 2010, even if you did not live with your RDP at the end of 2010.
- Your RDP died in 2010 and you did not re-register as an RDP or marry in 2010.
- Your RDP died in 2011 before you filed a 2010 tax return.

Married/RDP Filing Separately
- Community property rules apply to the division of income if you use the married/RDP filing separately status. For more information, get FTB Pub. 1031, Guidelines for Determining Resident Status, FTB Pub. 1051A, Guidelines for Married/RDP Filing Separate Returns, or FTB Pub. 1032, Tax Information for Military Personnel.
- You cannot claim a personal exemption credit for your RDP even if your RDP had no income, is not filing a tax return, and is not claimed as a dependent on another person's tax return.
- You may be able to file as head of household if your child lived with you and you lived apart from your RDP during the entire last six months of 2010.

Head of Household
For the specific requirements that must be met to qualify for head of household filing status, get FTB Pub. 1540, California Head of Household Filing Status. In general, head of household is for individuals who are unmarried and not in a registered domestic partnership and for certain married/RDP individuals living apart (considered unmarried or considered not in a registered domestic partnership) who provide a home for certain relatives. You may be entitled to use the head of household filing status as an RDP if all of the following apply:
- You met the requirements to be considered not in a registered domestic partnership on December 31, 2010.
- You paid more than one-half the cost of keeping up your home for the year 2010.
- For more than half the year, your home was the main home for you and your child who lived with you.
- You were not a nonresident alien at any time during the year.

For a child to qualify as your foster child for head of household purposes, the child must either be placed with you by an authorized placement agency or by order of a court. For more information, go to **ftb.ca.gov** and search for **hoh**.

Qualifying Widow(er) with Dependent Child
RDPs qualify for this filing status if **all** five of the following apply:
- Your RDP died in 2008 or 2009 and you did not marry or enter into another registered domestic partnership in 2010.
- You have a child, stepchild, adopted child, or foster child whom you claim as a dependent.
- This child lived in your home for all of 2010. Temporary absences, such as for vacation or school, count as time lived in the home.
- You paid over half the cost of keeping up your home for this child.
- You could have filed a joint return with your RDP the year he or she died, even if you actually did not do so.

Married/RDP Filing Separately

Division of Income – The domicile of the RDP earning the income determines the division of income between the RDPs when separate returns are filed. Each RDP must follow the laws of his or her state of domicile to determine if the income is separate or community property. California is a community property state. If the state of domicile is a community property state, when filing separate returns, each RDP must report half of the community property plus all separate income on his or her return. For California purposes, use federal Publication 555, Community Property, which contains an allocation worksheet to assist in the division of income.

If required to revise your federal adjusted gross income, have the following information available:

- Federal Income Tax Return and supporting schedules for each RDP.
- Copy of federal Form 1040 instructions including worksheets, as needed.
- If filing separately, a copy of FTB Pub. 1051A and allocation worksheet from federal Publication 555.

California Community/Separate Property

Community property is the total of the following property acquired and earnings received:

- By an RDP during a registered domestic partnership while domiciled in a community property state.
- By an RDP that is not separate property.

Each RDP owns one-half of all community property.

Separate property is:

- All property owned separately by an RDP before entering into a registered domestic partnership.
- All property acquired separately after entering into a registered domestic partnership, such as gifts, inheritances, and property purchased with separate funds.
- Money earned while domiciled in a separate property state.
- All property declared separate property in a valid agreement entered into before or after registration of the domestic partnership.

Community income is all income from community property, wages, salaries, and other compensation for personal services of either RDP while in a registered domestic partnership. Community income is divided equally between RDPs.

Under California law community status ends in any of the following situations:

- Upon the death of either RDP.
- When the decree of dissolution or termination of registered domestic partnership becomes final.
- When RDPs separate with no immediate intention of reconciliation.

Income from separate property is income of the RDP who owns the property.

When filing separate returns, the domicile of the RDP who earns the income determines the division of income between the RDPs. For income tax purposes, the income of RDPs domiciled in a community property state may be community income or separate income. When RDPs file separate returns, each RDP reports the following:

- One-half of the community income.
- All of his or her separate income.

For more information on community property, see federal Publication 555. RDPs will use the rules in federal Publication 555 for married people to determine how to apply those rules for California income tax purposes. The note in Publication 555 regarding California RDPs applies only to the filing of your federal return.

Pension Plans

For qualified pension plans, an RDP will not be treated as the spouse where such treatment would result in the disqualification for federal income tax purposes of a pension plan.

Anti-alienation provisions, applicable to qualified pension plans, prohibit assignment or transfer of plan assets except through a qualified domestic relations order (QDRO) or by certain survivor benefits. A QDRO is generally a court-ordered division of a qualified pension plan between spouses in relation to a divorce, a property division, or provision for child support. Because federal law does not recognize an RDP as a spouse, a plan will not be disqualified for California income tax purposes if a QDRO between RDPs is not recognized or if survivor benefits are not available to RDPs.

IRAs/Roth IRAs/Tax-Favored Accounts

An RDP will not be treated as a spouse where such treatment would result in a tax-favored account, such as a Individual Retirement Account (IRA), Roth IRA, Coverdell Education Savings Account (ESA), Archer Medical Savings Account (MSA), or IRC Section 529 plan (Qualified Tuition Program), no longer being qualified as a tax-favored account for federal purposes.

For example, under federal law, the beneficiary of a Coverdell ESA may transfer the remaining balance in an ESA to a new beneficiary. This new beneficiary must be "a member of the family," which is defined broadly to include the following relatives of the original beneficiary: spouse, child, brother, sister, stepbrother, stepsister, stepfather, stepmother, etc. Because federal law does not recognize an RDP as a spouse, the transfer of the balance in an ESA to a taxpayer's RDP or an RDP's child would result in the Coverdell ESA no longer being treated as a qualified tax-favored account for federal income tax purposes. Instead, the change in beneficiary would be considered a non-qualified distribution from the tax-favored account subject to additional tax of 10% for federal tax purposes and 2.5 % for California tax purposes. Therefore, for California purposes, an RDP would not be treated as a spouse for purposes of changing the beneficiary of a Coverdell ESA.

In the event of a distribution from an IRA, Roth IRA, or other tax-favored account, because federal law does not recognize RDPs, a taxpayer whose RDP or RDP's child receives distributions from the taxpayer's IRA, Roth IRA, or other tax-favored account, may incur additional tax penalties for federal income tax purposes, but not for California income tax purposes.

For example, in an IRA, if you take an early distribution from your IRA to pay the higher education expenses of your RDP or the child of your RDP, for federal purposes you would probably owe an additional tax of 10%, but for California purposes you would not owe the additional tax of 2.5%. However, for both federal and California tax purposes, you would need to include in your taxable income the early distribution from your IRA, unless you have a basis in the IRA that may be recovered tax-free.

For California income tax purposes, if you and/or your RDP is covered by an employer-provided retirement plan, then your California deduction for an IRA contribution may be limited. See the example for line 32 in the instructions for California RDP Adjustments Worksheet (included in this publication). The amount of a nondeductible IRA contribution creates a California-only IRA basis that is recoverable from IRA distributions that would otherwise be taxable for California income tax purposes. You must keep track of your California basis in your IRA. For general information about recovery of a California-only basis, get FTB Pub. 1005, Pension and Annuity Guidelines.

For California income tax purposes, if you or your RDP contributed to a Roth IRA in 2010 you need to review the income phase out limitations. The allowable Roth IRA contribution may be reduced based on you and your RDP's combined federal modified AGI.

2010 Filing Status	Federal Modified AGI
Married/RDP Filing Jointly or Qualifying Widow(er)	$167,000 - $177,000
Single, Head of Household, or Married/RDP filing separately and you did not live with your spouse/RDP for all of 2010	$105,000 - $120,000
Married/RDP Filing Separately and you lived with your spouse/RDP at any time in 2010	$0 - $10,000

Example:

Chris, Taxpayer One, and Pat, Taxpayer Two, are RDPs. Chris made a contribution to his Roth IRA of $5,000. Chris's federal modified AGI is $90,000. Pat made a contribution to his Roth IRA of $5,000. Pat's federal modified AGI is $95,000. Chris and Pat's combined federal AGI exceeds the $177,000 limitation for an allowable Roth IRA contribution. Because their combined federal modified AGI exceeds the limitation, for California purposes the Roth IRA contributions of Chris and Pat are treated as "excess contributions." However, California does not impose the six percent excise tax that is imposed under federal law on excess contributions to Roth IRAs.

If Chris or Pat receives a "qualified distribution" from a Roth IRA, the "qualified distribution" is tax-free and is not includible in their California taxable income. This tax-free treatment applies even if the "qualified distribution" includes earnings attributable to a previous "excess contribution" for California purposes.

Related Parties

In applying the IRC for California purposes:

- The definition of related parties includes RDPs. (IRC Section 267)

- The definition of spouse includes RDPs. Therefore, no gain or loss will be allowed for any transfer of property between RDPs. (IRC Section 1041)

- An RDP will be treated as a spouse for purposes of determining ownership of stock. However, if the treatment of an RDP as a spouse will lead to the disqualification of the taxpayer's choice of business entity, then the RDP will not be treated as a spouse for California purposes. (IRC Section 318)

California RDP Adjustments Worksheet —
TAXABLE YEAR
2010 Recalculated Federal Adjusted Gross Income

Name(s) as shown on return   SSN or ITIN

Part I Income Adjustment Worksheet Section A – Income		A Taxpayer One (taxable amounts from your original federal return)	B Taxpayer Two (taxable amounts from your original federal return)	C Adjustments	D Adjusted Federal Amounts (using the same rules applicable to spouses)
7 Wages, salaries, tips, etc	7				
8 Taxable interest. (b) TP1_____					
(b) TP2_____	(a)				
9 Ordinary dividends. (b) TP1_____					
(b) TP2_____	(a)				
10 Taxable refunds, credits, offsets of state and local income taxes	10				
11 Alimony received	11				
12 Business income or (loss)	12				
13 Capital gain or (loss)	13				
14 Other gains or (losses)	14				
15 IRA distributions. (a) TP1 _____ (a) TP2 _____	(b)				
16 Pensions and annuities. (a) TP1 _____ (a) TP2 _____	(b)				
17 Rental real estate, royalties, partnerships, S corporations, trusts, etc.	17				
18 Farm income or (loss)	18				
19 Unemployment compensation	19				
20 Social security benefits. (a) TP1 _____ (a) TP2 _____	(b)				
21 Other income	21				
22 Total. Combine line 7 through line 21 in column D. Go to Section B	22				
Section B – Adjustments to Income					
23 Educator expenses. CAUTION: See instructions	23				
24 Certain business expenses of reservists, performing artists, and fee-basis government officials	24				
25 Health savings account deduction	25				
26 Moving expenses	26				
27 One-half of self-employment tax	27				
28 Self-employed SEP, SIMPLE, and qualified plans	28				
29 Self-employed health insurance deduction	29				
30 Penalty on early withdrawal of savings	30				
31 Alimony paid	31				
32 IRA deduction	32				
33 Student loan interest deduction	33				
34 Tuition and fees deduction. CAUTION: See instructions	34				
35 Domestic production activities deduction	35				
36 Add line 23 through line 35 in column D	36				
37 Total. Subtract line 36 from line 22 in column D. Enter the amount here and on Form 540, 540A, or 540NR (Long and Short), line 13.	37				

Part II Adjustments to Federal Itemized Deductions

38   Federal itemized deductions. Add the amounts on each taxpayer's federal Schedule A (Form 1040),
      lines 4, 9, 15, 19, 20, 27, and 28. **Enter the amount here and on line 38, Schedule CA (540)** .... 38 _____

Note: Apply the 7.5% limitation rule to your federal adjusted gross income to arrive at the amount for line 4. Apply the 2% limitation rule to your adjusted gross income to arrive at the amount for line 27. There are other itemized deductions that are also subject to the 2% limitation rule and some itemized deductions are subject to an overall limitation rule. See federal Publication 17, Your Federal Income Tax, Part Five, Standard Deduction and Itemized Deductions.

8111103   CA RDP Adjustments Worksheet 2010

THIS PAGE INTENTIONALLY LEFT BLANK

Instructions for California RDP Adjustments Worksheet – Recalculated Federal Adjusted Gross Income

References to these instructions are to the Internal Revenue Code (IRC) as of **January 1, 2009**.

General Information

In general, for taxable years beginning on or after January 1, 2010, California law conforms to the Internal Revenue Code (IRC) as of January 1, 2009. However, there are continuing differences between California and federal law. When California conforms to federal tax law changes, we do not always adopt all of the changes made at the federal level. For more information, go to **ftb.ca.gov** and search for **conformity**. Additional information can be found in FTB Pub. 1001, Supplemental Guidelines to California Adjustments, the instructions for California Schedule CA (540 or 540NR), and the Business Entity tax booklets.

The instructions provided with California tax forms are a summary of California tax law and are only intended to aid taxpayers in preparing their state income tax returns. We include information that is most useful to the greatest number of taxpayers in the limited space available. It is not possible to include all requirements of the California Revenue and Taxation Code (R&TC) in the tax booklets. Taxpayers should not consider the tax booklets as authoritative law.

Purpose

Registered domestic partners (RDP) may use the California RDP Adjustments Worksheet or a pro forma federal Form 1040 to make RDP adjustments to calculate federal adjusted gross income (AGI) for California tax purposes.

To complete this worksheet, have the following information available:

- Federal Income Tax Return and supporting schedules for each RDP.
- Copy of federal Form 1040 Instructions including worksheets, as needed.
- If filing separately, a copy of federal Publication 555.
- If filing separately, a copy of FTB Pub. 1051A.

RDPs who file a California tax return and have no RDP adjustments between federal and California do not need to complete this worksheet. If you do not have any RDP adjustments, combine the amount on line 37 from each individual RDP's federal Form 1040 filed with the IRS and transfer the combined amount to Form 540, 540A, or 540NR (Long or Short), line 13.

RDP adjustments include but are not limited to the following:

- Division of community property, if not reported as community property on your federal tax return
- Capital losses
- Transactions between RDPs
- Sale of residence
- Dependent care assistance
- Investment interest
- Qualified residence acquisition loan & equity loan interest

- Expense depreciation property limitations
- Individual Retirement Account
- Education loan interest
- Rental real estate passive loss
- Rollover of publicly traded securities gain into specialized small business investment companies

RDPs filing as married/RDP filing jointly or married/RDP filing separately, and former RDPs filing single, with RDP adjustments will complete a pro forma federal Form 1040 using the same filing status as their California tax return or use this worksheet and instructions.

RDP adjustments occur when, for California purposes, you recalculate your federal tax return from a filing status of single or head of household to married/RDP filing jointly or married/RDP filing separately. RDP changes result in an increase or decrease to income or deductions. To complete this worksheet:

- Add column A and column B
- Add or subtract column C
- Enter the amount on column D
  (column A + column B) ± column C = column D

Example:
Chris, Taxpayer One, and Pat, Taxpayer Two, each have a capital loss on their separate federal tax returns, as shown below. Capital losses are limited to $3,000. When they recalculate their federal tax return as if married, they will make a $2,000 filing status adjustment in column C, line 13 of this worksheet. (A $3,000 loss plus a $2,000 loss equals a $5,000 loss; since they are limited to a $3,000 loss, the adjustment will be $2,000.)

Part I	Income Adjustments Worksheet Section A — Income		
13 Capital gain or (loss)			
A Taxpayer One	B Taxpayer Two	C Adjustments	D Adjusted Federal Amounts
($3,000)	($2,000)	$2,000	($3,000)

If Chris and Pat are filing separately, they are each limited to a $1,500 loss. Therefore, Chris will make a $1,500 filing status adjustment and Pat will make a $500 filing status adjustment on their separately filed tax returns. Because Chris and Pat are filing separately, each one is considered Taxpayer One as shown below.

Part II	Income Adjustments Worksheet Section A — Income		
13 Capital gain or (loss)			
A Taxpayer One	B Taxpayer Two	C Adjustments	D Adjusted Federal Amounts
($3,000)		$1,500	($1,500)
A Taxpayer One	B Taxpayer Two	C Adjustments	D Adjusted Federal Amounts
($2,000)		$500	($1,500)

CA RDP Adjustments Worksheet 2010 **Page 9**

Transfer Between Registered Domestic Partners

California conforms to IRC Section 1041, which provides that no gain or loss is recognized on transfers of property between spouses. For federal tax purposes, because federal law does not recognize RDPs, transfers between RDPs are not treated as transfers between spouses. However, beginning January 1, 2007, for California tax purposes, because California treats RDPs the same as spouses, no gain or loss is recognized on transfers of property between RDPs. This also applies to transfers between former RDPs, if the transfer is related to termination of the registered domestic partnership. For more information on transfers to a spouse, see Property Settlements in federal Publication 504, Divorced or Separated Individuals.

Instructions for Column A, Column B, and Column C

Column A – Taxpayer One Federal Form 1040

Taxpayer One, transfer the amounts from your federal Form 1040, line 7 through line 37 to column A of the worksheet.

Column B – Taxpayer Two Federal Form 1040

For married/RDP filing jointly taxpayer two, transfer the amounts from your federal Form 1040, line 7 through line 37 to column B of the worksheet.

For married/RDP filing separately or former RDP filing single, no amount will be shown in column B. All adjustments for community property will be made in column C.

For more information on community property, see federal Publication 555. RDPs will use the rules in federal Publication 555 for married people to determine how to apply those rules for California income tax purposes. The note in Publication 555 regarding California RDPs applies to filing of your federal tax return.

Column C – Adjustments

Use column C to make California RDP adjustments on line 7 through line 21 and line 23 through line 35 following the specific line instructions below. For additional information use the federal Form 1040 instructions. If the amount is less than zero (negative), enter the result in parentheses. For example: (12,345).

Part I, Income Adjustment Worksheet

Section A – Income, Columns A, B, and C

Line 7 – Wages, salaries, tips, etc.

Enter the total of your wages, salaries, tips, etc. For most people, the amount to enter on this line should be shown on box 1 of their Forms(s) W-2.

For additional information see the federal Form 1040 instructions for line 7.

Adjustments:

Exclusion for medical expenses reimbursement

California allows an exclusion from gross income for employer-provided accident or health insurance, and medical expense reimbursement for RDPs and their partner's dependents if they were not previously deducted. Self-employed individuals may also claim a deduction for health insurance costs paid for themselves, their spouse or RDP, and their dependent(s), including the dependent(s) of their RDP. Enter the amount included in federal income as a negative number on line 7, column C.

Dependent care assistance programs (IRC Section 129)

The amount which may be excluded for dependent care assistance with respect to dependent care services provided during a taxable year shall not exceed $5,000 ($2,500 in the case of a separate tax return filed by a married/RDP individual).

For married/RDP filing jointly, if you and your RDP excluded more than $5,000 on your federal tax returns, your federal adjusted gross income for California purposes is increased by the amount which exceeds $5,000. For married/RDP filing separately, if you excluded more than $2,500 on your federal tax return, your federal adjusted gross income for California purposes is increased by the amount which exceeds $2,500.

Line 8a – Taxable interest

Each payer should send you a Form 1099-INT, Interest Income, or Form 1099-OID, Original Issue Discount. Enter your total taxable interest income on line 8a.

For additional information see the federal Form 1040 instructions for line 8a.

Line 8b – Tax-exempt interest

If you received any tax-exempt interest, such as from municipal bonds, each payer should send you a Form 1099-INT. Enter the total on line 8b.

For additional information see the federal Form 1040 instructions for line 8b.

Line 9a – Ordinary dividends

Each payer should send you a Form 1099-DIV, Dividends and Distributions. Enter your total ordinary dividends on line 9a.

For additional information see the federal Form 1040 instructions for line 9a.

Line 9b – Qualified dividends

Enter your total qualified dividends on line 9b.

For additional information see the federal Form 1040 instructions for line 9b.

Line 10 – Taxable refunds, credits, offsets of state and local income taxes

If you received a refund, credit, or offset of state or local income taxes in 2010, you may receive a Form 1099-G, Certain Government Payments.

For additional information see the federal Form 1040 instructions for line 10.

Line 11 – Alimony received

Enter amounts received as alimony or separate maintenance.

For additional information see the federal Form 1040 instructions for line 11.

Adjustment: If you are an RDP receiving alimony not included in your federal income, enter the alimony amount on line 11, column C.

Line 12 – Business income or (loss)
Enter your business income or loss.

For additional information see the federal Form 1040 instructions for line 12.

Adjustments:

Election to treat certain depreciable business assets as an expense (IRC Section 179(b))
You may elect to treat the cost of any IRC Section 179 property as an expense, which is not chargeable to capital account. Any cost so treated shall be allowed as a deduction for the taxable year in which the IRC Section 179 property is placed in service.

If you are filing married/RDP filing separately, your deduction is limited to 50% of the total allowable. Enter 50% of the total deduction as a positive number on line 12, column C.

Election to treat certain reforestation expenditures as an expense (IRC Section 194)
In the case of any qualified timber property with respect to which the taxpayer has made an election, the taxpayer shall treat reforestation expenditures that are paid or incurred during the taxable year with respect to such property as an expense that is not chargeable to capital account. The reforestation expenditures shall be allowed as a deduction. The aggregate amount of reforestation expenditures, with respect to each qualified timber property, shall not exceed $10,000 ($5,000 if you file as married/RDP filing separately).

If you claimed a reforestation expense deduction in the amount of $5,000 on your federal tax return and you are filing married/RDP filing jointly, enter the difference between your total reforestation expense (up to $10,000 for each qualified timber property) and the amount you deducted on your federal tax return on line 12, column C, as a negative number.

Rollover of publicly traded securities gain into specialized small business investment companies (IRC Section 1044)
In the case of the sale or any publicly traded securities with respect to which the taxpayer elects the application of IRC Section 1044, gain from such sale shall be recognized only to the extent that the amount realized on such sale exceeds the cost of any common stock or partnership interest in a specialized small business investment company purchased by the taxpayer during the 60-day period beginning on the date of such sale, reduced by any portion of such cost previously taken into account under this section.

The amount of gain that may be excluded for any taxable year shall not exceed the lesser of $50,000 ($25,000 if filing married/RDP filing separately) or $500,000 ($250,000 if filing married/RDP filing separately), reduced by the amount of gain excluded for all preceding taxable years. If you are filing married/RDP filing jointly, enter the difference between your single tax return and your recalculated amounts (not to exceed the limitations) on line 12, column C, as a negative number.

Line 13 – Capital gain or (loss) (IRC Section 1044(b)(3))
If you had a capital gain or loss, including any capital gain distributions or a capital loss carryover from 2009, you must complete and attach federal Schedule D (Form 1040), Capital Gains and Losses.

For additional information see the federal Form 1040 instructions for line 13.

Adjustment: For California purposes, RDPs are treated as husband and wife in provisions where the husband and wife are treated as one person. RDPs are not treated as one person at the federal level.

If your capital losses are more than your capital gains, you can claim a capital loss deduction. The capital loss deduction for RDPs who file as married/RDP filing jointly is limited to $3,000 ($1,500 if you are an RDP filing as married/RDP filing separately).

Line 14 – Other gains or (losses) (IRC Section 121)
If you sold or exchanged assets used in a trade or business, see the Instructions for federal Form 4797, Sale of Business Property.

Adjustment: RDPs are allowed an exclusion of gain on the sale of their principal residence. RDPs filing as married/RDP filing jointly are able to exclude up to $500,000 ($250,000 if you file as married/RDP filing separately).

If you sold your principal residence and excluded a gain of $250,000 on your federal tax return and are filing married/RDP filing jointly, enter the difference between your total gain (up to $500,000) and the amount you excluded from your federal income on line 14, column C, as a negative number.

Line 15 – IRA distributions
An RDP will not be treated as a spouse where such treatment would result in a tax-favored account not being qualified as a tax-favored account for federal income tax purposes.

Adjustment: An RDP may have an adjustment to line 15 if the RDP has a California-only basis in an IRA, which is recoverable from an IRA distribution. For example, an RDP may have a California-only basis in an IRA if the RDP's partner is covered by an employer-provided retirement plan. Based on the RDPs' combined adjusted gross income, the available deduction for an IRA contribution may be reduced for California income tax purposes. The amount disallowed for an IRA contribution on this worksheet creates a California-only basis in the IRA. RDPs must keep track of their California-only basis in order to recover it tax-free from IRA distributions reported on line 15 in future years.

Line 15a and Line 15b – IRA distributions
You should receive a Form 1099-R, Distribution From Pensions, Annuities, Retirement or Profit-Sharing Plans, IRAs, Insurance Contracts, etc., showing the amount of any distribution from your IRA. Unless otherwise noted in the line 15a and line 15b instructions, an IRA includes a traditional IRA, Roth IRA, simplified employee pension (SEP) IRA, and a savings incentive match plan for employees (SIMPLE) IRA. Except as provided in the federal Form 1040 instructions for line 15a and line 15b, leave

line 15a blank and enter the total distribution on line 15b.

For additional information see the federal Form 1040 instructions for line 15a and line 15b.

Line 16a and Line 16b – Pensions and annuities
You should receive a Form 1099-R showing the amount of your pension and annuity payments.

For additional information see the federal Form 1040 instructions for line 16a and line 16b.

Line 17 – Rental real estate, royalties, partnerships, S corporations, trust, etc.
Enter the amount from federal Schedule E (Form 1040), Supplemental Income and Loss, line 26 or line 41, here.

Adjustment: Get federal Form 8582, Passive Activity Loss Limitations, if your modified AGI is over $100,000. If you or your RDP actively participated in a passive rental real estate activity, you can deduct up to $25,000 of loss from the activity from your nonpassive income. This special allowance is an exception to the general rule disallowing losses in excess of income from passive activities. The maximum amount of the special allowance is reduced if your modified AGI is more than $100,000 ($50,000 if you file as married/RDP filing separately).

If you have a loss, subtract the total allowable loss shown on your recalculated federal Form 8582 from the total of the amounts on line 17, column A and column B. Enter the result on line 17, column C, as a positive number.

Line 18 – Farm income or (loss)
Enter the amount from federal Schedule F (Form 1040), Profit or Loss From Farming, line 36 here.

Adjustment: Election to treat certain depreciable business assets as an expense (IRC Section 179(b))
You may elect to treat the cost of any IRC Section 179 property as an expense, which is not chargeable to capital account. Any cost so treated shall be allowed as a deduction for the taxable year in which the IRC Section 179 property is placed in service.

If you are filing as married/RDP filing separately, your deduction is limited to 50% of the total allowable. Enter 50% of the total deduction as a positive number on line 18, column C.

Line 19 – Unemployment compensation
You should receive a Form 1099-G showing the total unemployment compensation paid to you in 2010.

For additional information see the federal Form 1040 instructions for line 19.

Line 20a and Line 20b – Social security benefits
You should receive a Form SSA-1099, Social Security Benefit Statement, showing in box 3 the total social security benefits paid to you.

For additional information see the federal Form 1040 instructions for line 20.

Adjustment: A portion of your benefits may be taxable. How much is taxable depends on the total amount of your benefits and other income. Generally, the higher that total amount, the greater the taxable part of your benefits. To figure the total taxable amount of your social security benefits, calculate the taxable benefit amount using the Social Security Benefits Worksheet found in the federal Form 1040 instructions. Subtract that amount from the total of the amounts on line 20, combine column A and column B on your California RDP Adjustment Worksheet. Enter the result on line 20, column C.

Line 21 – Other income
Use line 21 to report any income not reported elsewhere on your tax return or other schedules.

For additional information see the federal Form 1040 instructions for line 21.

Section B – Adjustments to Income, Columns A, B, and C

Line 23 – Educator expenses
The deduction for educator expenses that was taken on this line of the 2009 federal Form 1040 has expired and does not apply for 2010. The line has been reserved in case Congress extends the deduction to 2010. To find out whether Congress has extended the deduction, go to **irs.gov**.

Line 24 – Certain business expenses of reservists, performing artists, and fee-basis government officials
Include the following deductions on line 24:

- Certain business expenses of National Guard and reserve members who traveled more than 100 miles from home to perform services as a National Guard or reserve member.
- Performing-arts-related expenses.
- Business expenses of fee-basis state or local government officials.

For additional information see the federal Form 1040 instructions for line 24.

Adjustment: RDPs may only claim expenses as a performing artist if they file as married/RDP filing jointly, unless they lived apart from their RDP for the entire year.

Line 25 – Health savings account (HSA) deduction
If contributions (other than employer contributions) were made to your HSA for 2010, you may be able to take this deduction. See federal Form 8889, Health Savings Accounts (HSAs), for additional information.

A "tax-favored account" means an individual account, plan, or arrangement that is exempt from tax under federal law, including a HSA. Where the treatment of an RDP as a spouse would result in a tax-favored account that would not be qualified as a tax-favored account for federal income tax purposes, the RDP will not be treated as a spouse for California tax purposes with respect to that account.

Line 26 – Moving expenses
If you moved in connection with your job or business or started a new job, you may be able to take this deduction.

For additional information see the federal Form 1040 instructions for line 26.

Line 27 – One-half of self-employment tax
If you were self-employed and owe self-employment tax, use federal Schedule SE, Self Employment Tax, to figure the amount of your deduction.

Line 28 – Self-employed SEP, SIMPLE, and qualified plans
If you were self-employed or a partner, you may be able to take this deduction. See federal Publication 560, Retirement Plans for Small Business (SEP, SIMPLE, and

Qualified Plans), or, if you were a minister, see federal Publication 517, Social Security and Other Information for Members of the Clergy and Religious Workers.

Line 29 – Self-employed health insurance deduction
You may be able to deduct the amount you paid for health insurance coverage (established under your business) for yourself, your RDP, your dependents, and your RDP's dependents. Your total California deduction cannot exceed the limitations explained in the federal instructions. Do not include health insurance costs for any month you were eligible to participate in any subsidized health plan maintained by your or your domestic partner's employer.

For additional information see the federal Form 1040 instructions for line 29.

Adjustments:

Self-employed health insurance deduction
Enter the amount of health insurance coverage for your registered domestic partner and their dependents on line 29, column C, as a positive amount.

Subsidized health plan maintained by your partner's employer
Enter the amount of health insurance cost included for any month you were eligible to participate in any subsidized health plan maintained by your registered domestic partner's employer on line 29, column C, as a negative amount.

Line 30 – Penalty on early withdrawal of savings
The Form 1099-INT or Form 1099-OID you received will show the amount of any penalty you were charged.

Line 31 – Alimony paid
If you made payments to or for your spouse/RDP or former spouse/RDP under a divorce or separation instrument, you may be able to take this deduction. For additional information, see federal Publication 504.

Adjustment: If you are an RDP paying alimony not included in your adjustment to income for federal purposes, enter the alimony amount on line 31, column C, as a positive amount.

Line 32 – IRA deduction
If you made contributions to a traditional IRA for 2010, you may be able to take an IRA deduction.

For additional information see the federal Form 1040 instructions for line 32.

Adjustment: If you are an RDP and your federal modified AGI exceeds the amounts in the charts below, your IRA deduction will be limited. To figure your adjustment, see federal Form 1040 instructions for line 32. Enter the adjustment amount on line 32, column C, as a positive amount.

A "tax-favored account" means an individual account, plan, or arrangement that is exempt from tax under federal law, including an IRA. Where the treatment of an RDP as a spouse would result in a tax-favored account that would not be qualified as a tax-favored account for federal income tax purposes, the RDP would not be treated as a spouse for California tax purposes with respect to that account.

Use the chart below if the RDP that contributed to an IRA was covered by an employer retirement plan.

2010 Filing Status	Federal modified AGI
Married/RDP Filing Jointly or Qualifying Widow(er)	$89,000 - $109,000
Single, Head of Household, or Married/RDP filing separately and you did not live with your spouse/RDP for all of 2010	$56,000 - $66,000
Married/RDP Filing Separately and you lived with your spouse/RDP at any time in 2010	$0 - $10,000

Use the chart below if the RDP that contributed to an IRA was **not** covered by an employer plan, but the partner of the RDP was covered by an employer retirement plan.

2010 Filing Status	Federal modified AGI
Married/RDP Filing Jointly or Qualifying Widow(er)	$167,000 - $177,000
Single, Head of Household, or Married/RDP filing separately and you did not live with your spouse/RDP for all of 2010	$ no phase-out
Married/RDP Filing Separately and you lived with your spouse/RDP at any time in 2010	$0 - $10,000

Example:
Chris, Taxpayer One, and Pat, Taxpayer Two, are RDPs. Chris made an IRA contribution of $5,000 in 2010. Chris's federal modified AGI is $80,000, he is not covered by an employer-provided pension plan. On his separate federal tax return, Chris deducted his entire IRA contribution on line 32 of his Form 1040. Pat is covered by an employer-provided pension plan and he did not make an IRA contribution in 2010. Pat's federal modified AGI is $150,000. Chris and Pat's combined federal modified AGI exceeds the $177,000 limitation and they cannot deduct an IRA contribution. When they recalculate their federal modified AGI, as if married, they will make a $5,000 filing status adjustment in column C, line 32 of this worksheet.

Part I	Income Adjustments Worksheet Section B – Adjustments to Income		
Line 32 IRA Deduction			
A. Taxpayer One	B. Taxpayer Two	C. Adjustments	D. Adjusted Federal Amounts
($5,000)	$0	$5,000	$0

Line 33 – Student loan interest deduction
Use the Student Loan Interest Deduction Worksheet in the federal Form 1040 instructions to determine your student loan interest deduction.

For additional information see the federal Form 1040 instructions for line 33.

Line 34 – Tuition and fees deduction

The tuition and fees deduction that was taken on this line of the 2009 federal Form 1040 has expired and does not apply for 2010. The line has been reserved in case Congress extends the deduction to 2010. To find out whether Congress has extended the deduction, go to **irs.gov**.

Line 35 – Domestic production activities deduction

You may be able to deduct up to six percent of your qualified production activities income.

For additional information see the federal Form 1040 instructions for line 35.

Instructions for Column D

Column D – Adjusted Federal Amounts

To calculate column D:

- Add column A and column B
- Add or subtract column C
- Enter the amount in column D

   (column A + column B) ± column C = column D

Line 22 – Total

Combine line 7 through line 21 in column D.

Line 36

Add line 23 through 35 in column D.

Line 37 – Total

Subtract line 36, column D from line 22, column D. Enter the amount here and on Form 540, 540A, or 540NR (Long or Short), line 13.

Transfer the amounts from column D, line 7 through line 37 to Schedule CA, column A, line 7 through line 37.

Part II Adjustments to Federal Itemized Deductions

Line 38 – Federal itemized deductions

The following adjustments may be required for qualified residence interest (IRC Section 163(h)):

- **Acquisition indebtedness** – The aggregate amount treated as acquisition indebtedness for a period shall not exceed $1,000,000 ($500,000 in the case of a married individual or an RDP filing a separate tax return). If your combined acquisition indebtedness is over $1,000,000, enter the amount of interest on your indebtedness (up to $1,000,000) on your recalculated federal Schedule A (Form 1040), line 10 or line 11.

- **Home equity indebtedness** – The aggregate amount treated as home equity indebtedness for any period shall not exceed $100,000 ($50,000 in the case of a married individual or an RDP filing a separate tax return). If your combined home equity indebtedness

is over $100,000 enter the amount of interest on your indebtedness (up to $100,000) on your recalculated federal Schedule A (Form 1040), line 10 or line 11.

Medical and Dental Expenses

Taxpayer benefits are extended to include the taxpayer's RDP and their dependent(s) for medical expenses and health insurance benefits.

Combine your medical and dental expenses and apply the 7.5% limitation rule to your recalculated jointly adjusted gross income to arrive at the amount for line 4 of the federal Schedule A (Form 1040).

Job Expenses and Certain Miscellaneous Deductions

Combine your job expenses and miscellaneous deductions and apply the two percent limitation rule to your recalculated jointly adjusted gross income to arrive at the amount for line 27 of the federal Schedule A (Form 1040).

Frequently Asked Questions

(For more RDP information, go to **ftb.ca.gov** and search for **rdp.**)

1. **Can I file a joint California tax return with my RDP for tax years prior to 2007?**

   No. Domestic partners **cannot** file a married filing joint or married filing separate tax return for tax years prior to 2007. A domestic partner is required to use the same filing status for state income tax purposes that was used or would have been used for federal income tax purposes. For taxable years beginning on or after January 1, 2007, domestic partners are required to use the same filing status available to married persons.

2. **Is the earned income of domestic partners treated as community property for tax years prior to 2007?**

   No. Earned income is not treated as community property for state income tax purposes for tax years prior to 2007.

3. **If one RDP dies, can the surviving RDP file a joint tax return?**

   Yes, if an RDP dies, the surviving RDP can file as married/RDP filing jointly for the year the RDP dies if he or she does not enter into a new registered domestic partnership or marriage. If an RDP dies in the following year prior to filing their tax return the surviving RDP can file a married/RDP filing jointly tax return. For more information on deceased taxpayers, go to **ftb.ca.gov** and search for **deceased taxpayer**.

4. **Can the Franchise Tax Board (FTB) waive accuracy-related penalties for RDPs due to reasonable cause?**

   Yes, but there are no special rules to grant waiver of penalties for RDPs. "Reasonable cause" is a standard exception to most penalties imposed under the California Revenue and Taxation Code and the federal Internal Revenue Code. Generally, reasonable cause exists where the failure to comply occurs despite the exercise of ordinary business care and prudence.

5. **Do mortgage interest rules for RDPs filing California tax returns apply?**

   Yes, but only if the limitations applicable on a federal tax return for married individuals would limit your interest deduction on your California return. For more information about those limits see federal Publication 936, Home Mortgage Interest Deduction.

6. **Can an RDP who files a California married/RDP filing jointly tax return exclude up to $500,000 of capital gain on the sale of a principal residence?**

   Yes, if they meet the capital gain exclusion rules that apply to a married individual filing a joint tax return. For more information, see federal Publication 523, Selling Your Home.

7. **Can an RDP who filed a joint tax return apply for relief under California's innocent joint filer provisions?**

   Yes, California innocent joint filer provisions apply to anyone who files a married/RDP filing joint tax return. For more information, get FTB Pub. 705, Innocent Joint Filer – Relief From Paying California Income Taxes.

8. **If a court orders termination of a registered domestic partnership and a California Family Law Court awards spousal support (alimony), what is the tax treatment of these payments?**

   For California, if the payment satisfies the requirements under tax law for alimony, it would be deducted by the payor and included by the payee. However, federal treatment of these payments is uncertain.

9. **If a court with jurisdiction of a dissolution proceeding for a registered domestic partnership assigns a tax debt owing to the FTB to one of the partners, is the FTB bound by the court order?**

   The parties to a dissolution can stipulate to any payment arrangement of taxes that they wish, and the court could order one party to satisfy outstanding tax liabilities. However, the FTB is not generally bound by such a court order. There are some circumstances where the FTB will follow a court order revising tax liability between the parties to a dissolution proceeding. For more information, get FTB Pub. 705.

10. **Can an RDP file as "head of household" (HOH) on a California tax return?**

    Yes, RDPs can file as a HOH on a California tax return if he or she maintains the main home for his or her birth child, stepchild, adopted child, or eligible foster child and are "considered not in a registered domestic partnership."

    To be "considered not in a registered domestic partnership" you must meet **all** of the following requirements:

    - Your RDP did not live in your home during the last six months of the tax year.
    - You file a separate tax return.
    - You pay more than half the cost of keeping up your home for the tax year.
    - Your home was the main home of your birth child, stepchild, adopted child, or eligible foster child for more than half the year.
    - You must be able to claim an exemption for the child.

    For more information on filing HOH, get FTB Pub. 1540, California Head of Household Filing Status.

Definitions

Registered Domestic Partnership – Two persons who filed a Declaration of Domestic Partnership with the California Secretary of State.

Marriage – A legal union of two persons.

Married – United in a legally recognized marriage.

Spouse – A married person or a person who is part of a lawful marriage.

Former Spouse – A former married person or a person who was previously part of a legal marriage.

Married/RDP Filing Jointly Filing Status – A filing status for married couples who were married as of the last day of the tax year. Beginning in 2007, this filing status may also be used by RDPs who have registered as domestic partners with the California Secretary of State by the last day of the tax year.

Married/RDP Filing Separately Filing Status – A filing status for married couples and RDPs who choose to report their respective incomes, exemptions, and deductions on separate tax returns.

Divorce – The legal termination of a marriage.

Unmarried/Not in a Registered Domestic Partnership – A taxpayer is unmarried and not in a registered domestic partnership if on the last day of the tax year, one of the following applies:

- The taxpayer has never been married and never entered into a registered domestic partnership.

- The taxpayer is legally divorced from his or her spouse/RDP under a final decree of divorce or a final decree of dissolution of RDP. A petition for divorce or dissolution of RDP **or** an interlocutory decree of divorce or interlocutory decree of RDP is **not** the same as a final decree. A married taxpayer remains married or an RDP until the final decree is issued.

- The taxpayer is legally separated from his or her spouse/RDP under a final decree of legal separation. A petition for legal separation or an informal separation agreement is **not** the same as a final decree of legal separation. Also, simply living apart from a spouse/RDP is **not** the same as being legally separated under a final decree of legal separation.

A married/RDP taxpayer is unmarried or not in an RDP for head of household purposes if the taxpayer's spouse/RDP was a nonresident alien at any time during the year. However, if the taxpayer filed a joint tax return in a previous year by choosing to treat the spouse/RDP as a resident, the choice continues in subsequent tax years until it is revoked. If the taxpayer has not revoked the choice by the extended due date for filing a tax return in the current year, the nonresident alien spouse/RDP is still a resident for tax purposes in the current year and the taxpayer remains married or an RDP.

Considered Unmarried (Head of Household) – To qualify for head of household filing status, a married taxpayer or RDP must meet the requirements to be considered unmarried or considered not in a registered domestic partnership. One of those requirements is that the taxpayer's spouse or partner must not have lived in the home at any time during the last six months of the tax year.

Decree of Dissolution – The Final Judgment of Divorce (also referred to as a Decree of Dissolution or Decree of Divorce); the court order that terminates a marriage and certain registered domestic partnerships. The marriage or registered domestic partnership is not officially terminated until a final decree is issued by the court.

Legal Separation – To be legally separated, a person must have received a final decree of legal separation issued by a court. A petition for legal separation, an informal separation agreement, or simply living apart from a spouse/RDP is not the same as being legally separated under a final decree of legal separation.

Termination/Dissolution of RDP – Depending on the circumstances, registered domestic partnerships may be terminated either by court order following a dissolution proceeding in the Superior Court or by filing a Notice of Termination of Domestic Partnership with the California Secretary of State.

Mother – A female parent that has born an offspring, has adopted a child, or otherwise established a maternal relationship with another person.

Father – A male parent who functions in a paternal capacity with regard to another; especially, a man who adopts a child.

Parent – A father or mother.

Additional Information

How to Get California Tax Information

By Internet – You can download, view, and print California tax forms and publications at **ftb.ca.gov**.

By phone – To order California tax forms, call our automated phone service at 800.338.0505.

In person – Many libraries and post offices provide free California tax booklets during the filing season.

Employees at libraries and post offices cannot provide tax information or assistance.

By mail – We will send you two copies of each tax form and one copy of each set of instructions. Allow two weeks to receive your order. If you live outside California allow three weeks to receive your order. Write to:

TAX FORMS REQUEST UNIT
FRANCHISE TAX BOARD
PO BOX 307
RANCHO CORDOVA CA   95741-0307

Letters

If you write to us, be sure your letter includes your social security number (SSN) or Individual Taxpayer Identification Number (ITIN), and your daytime and evening telephone numbers. Send your letter to:

FRANCHISE TAX BOARD
PO BOX 942840
SACRAMENTO CA   94240-0040

We will respond to your letter within ten weeks. In some cases, we may need to call you for additional information.

Volunteer Income Tax Assistance (VITA)

At more than 1,200 sites throughout California, trained volunteers provide free assistance to low-income, senior, disabled, and non-English speaking persons who need to file simple federal and state income tax returns. Many military bases also provide this service for members of the armed forces.

The locations for VITA will be listed at **ftb.ca.gov** from mid-January 2011, through April 15, 2011, or call the Franchise Tax Board at 800.852.5711 to find the volunteer assistance location nearest you.

Telephone Assistance

Telephone assistance is available year-round from 7 a.m. until 5 p.m. Monday through Friday, except holidays. Hours are subject to change.

Telephone: 800.852.5711 from within the United States
916.845.6500 from outside the United States
800.829.1040 for federal tax questions,
call the IRS

TTY/TDD: 800.822.6268 for persons with hearing or
speech impairments

Asistencia bilingüe en español

Asistencia telefónica está disponible todo el año durante las 7 a.m. y las 5 p.m. lunes a viernes, excepto días festivos. Las horas están sujetas a cambios.

Teléfono: 800.852.5711 dentro de los Estados Unidos
916.845.6500 fuera de los Estados Unidos
800.829.1040 para preguntas sobre
impuestos federales

TTY/TDD: 800.822.6268 personas con discapacidades
auditivas y del habla

Sitio web: **ftb.ca.gov**

www.ingramcontent.com/pod-product-compliance
Lightning Source LLC
Chambersburg PA
CBHW051226200326
41519CB00025B/7266